speak to us of **love**

OSHO

Extemporaneous talks given by Osho at the
OSHO International Meditation Resort, Pune, India

speak to us of **love**

Selected talks by Osho on Kahlil Gibran's *The Prophet*

OSHO

Published by OSHO Media International

Originally published as *The Messiah,* in 2 vols

Ten selected talks by Osho, given to a live audience. All of Osho's talks have been
published in full as books, and are also available as original audio recordings. Audio
recordings and the complete text archive can be found via the online OSHO Library at
www.osho.com/library

"On Children", "On Love", "On Marriage", "On Giving", "On Freedom",
"On Friendship", "On Work", "On Pleasure" from THE PROPHET by Kahlil Gibran,
copyright 1923 by Kahlil Gibran and renewed 1951 by Administrators C.T.A. of Kahlil
Gibran Estate and Mary G. Gibran. Used by permission of Alfred A. Knopf, a division
of Random House, Inc.

OSHO MEDIA INTERNATIONAL
New York • Zurich • Mumbai
an imprint of
OSHO INTERNATIONAL
www.osho.com/oshointernational

Distributed by Publishers Group Worldwide
www.pgw.com

Library of Congress Catalog-In-Publication Data is available

Print edition: ISBN-13: 978-0-918963-98-7

Printed in China

contents

preface

Kahlil Gibran is pure music, a mystery, such that only poetry can sometimes grasp, but only sometimes.

Centuries have passed; there have been great men, but Kahlil Gibran is a category in himself. I cannot conceive that even in the future there is a possibility of another man of such deep insight into the human heart, into the unknown that surrounds us.

He has done something impossible. He has been able to bring at least a few fragments of the unknown into human language. He has raised human language and human consciousness as no other man has ever done. Through Kahlil Gibran, it seems all the mystics, all the poets, all creative souls have joined hands and shared themselves.

Although he has been immensely successful in reaching people, still he feels it is not the whole truth, but just a glimpse. But to see the glimpse of truth is a beginning of a pilgrimage that leads you to the ultimate, to the absolute, to the universal.

There are a few things I would like to say to you before I make my commentaries on the statements of Kahlil Gibran.

First, he is certainly a great poet, perhaps the greatest that has ever been born on the earth, but he is not a mystic; and there is a tremendous difference between a poet and a mystic. The poet, once in a while, suddenly finds himself in the same space as the mystic. In those rare moments, roses shower over him. On those rare occasions, he is almost a Gautam Buddha – but remember, I'm saying *almost*.

These rare moments come and go. He's not the master of those rare moments. They come like the breeze and the fragrance and by the time you have become aware they are gone.

A poet's genius is that he catches those moments in words. Those moments come into your life too. They are free gifts of existence – or in other words, glimpses to provoke in you a search, a desire to come to a moment when this space will become your very life, your blood, your bones, your marrow. You will breathe it; your heart will beat it. You will never be able to lose it, even if you want to.

The poet is for moments a mystic, and the mystic is a poet forever.

But this has always created a very difficult question, and nobody has been able to solve it. The problem has been posed again and again, thousands of times all over the world: if the poet gets only glimpses yet creates so much beauty, so much poetry – words start becoming alive the moment he touches them – why have the mystics not been able to produce the same kind of poetry? They are twenty-four hours a day, day and night, in that creative state, but their words don't carry that beauty. Even the words of Gautam Buddha or Jesus Christ fall very much short of the words of people like Kahlil Gibran, Mikhail Naimy, Rabindranath Tagore. It certainly seems to be strange, because the people who have only *moments* create so much and the people who have the universal consciousness available to them, waking or sleeping... What happens? Why have they not been able to produce Kahlil Gibrans? And nobody has answered it.

My own experience is that if a beggar finds a gold mine, he will sing and he will dance and he will go mad with joy – but not an emperor.

A poet once in a while becomes an emperor – but only once in a while; that's why he cannot take it for granted. But the mystic is not just for a moment merged with the universal consciousness – he *is* merged. There is no way of coming back.

Those small glimpses may be translated into words because they are only dewdrops. But the mystic has become the ocean; hence, silence becomes his song. All words seem so impotent, nothing seems to be capable of bringing his experience into any kind of communication. And the ocean is so vast and he is continuously one with it; naturally, he himself forgets that he is separate.

To create, you have to be there to create. To sing a song, you have to be there. But the mystic has become the song. His presence is his poetry. You cannot print it, you cannot paint it, you can only drink it.

To communicate with a poet is one thing, but to be in communion with a mystic is totally different. But it is good to begin with poets, because if you are not able even to absorb dewdrops, the ocean is not for you. Or, better to say, you are not for the ocean. To you, even the dewdrop will appear like a vast ocean.

Kahlil Gibran has written almost thirty books. *The Prophet*, which we are going to discuss, is his first book; the remaining are rubbish. This is a strange phenomenon – what happened to the man? When he wrote this he was just young, twenty-one years of age. One would have thought that now more and more would be coming. And he tried hard; he was writing his whole life, but nothing came even close to the beauty and the truth of *The Prophet*. Perhaps the window never opened again.

A poet is accidentally mystic. It is just by accident: a breeze comes, you cannot produce it. And because he became world famous – this is one book which must have been translated in almost all the languages of the world – he tried hard to do something better, and that's where he failed. It is unfortunate that he never came across a man who could have told him a simple truth: "You had not tried when you created *The Prophet*, it *happened*. And now you are trying to *do* it.

"It has happened; it is not your doing. You may have been a vehicle. Something that was not yours…" – just like a child is born of a mother.

The mother cannot create the child, she is simply a passage. *The Prophet* belongs to the category of a very small number of books which are not dependent on your action, your intelligence, on you; on the contrary, they are possible only when you are not, when you allow them to happen, when you don't stand in the way. You are so relaxed that you don't interfere.

This is one of those rarest of books. In it, you will not find Kahlil Gibran – that's the beauty of the book. He allowed the universe to flow through him; he is simply a medium, a passage, just a hollow bamboo which does not hinder the flute player.

In my experience, books like *The Prophet* are holier than your so-called holy books. And because these books are authentically holy, they have not created a religion around themselves. They don't give you any ritual, they don't give you any discipline, they don't give you any commandments. They simply allow you to have a glimpse of the same experience which happened to them.

The whole experience cannot come into words, but something – perhaps not the whole rose, but a few petals... They are enough proof that a rose exists. Your window has just to be open, so a breeze sometimes can bring petals.

Those petals coming through a breeze into your being are really invitations of the unknown. Existence is calling you for a long pilgrimage. Unless that pilgrimage is made you will remain meaningless, dragging somehow, but not really living. You will not have laughter in your heart.

Kahlil Gibran avoids his own name by creating a fictitious name, Almustafa. That's the beginning of *The Prophet*. Almustafa is the prophet.

Great truths can only be said in parables.

Osho
Reflections on Kahlil Gibran's The Prophet

LOVE
speak to us of love

Then said Almitra, Speak to us of Love.
And he raised his head and looked upon the people, and there fell a
stillness upon them. And with a great voice he said:
When love beckons to you, follow him,
Though his ways are hard and steep.
And when his wings enfold you yield to him,
Though the sword hidden among his pinions may wound you.
And when he speaks to you believe in him,
Though his voice may shatter your dreams as the north wind lays
waste the garden.
For even as love crowns you so shall he crucify you. Even as he is for
your growth so is he for your pruning.
Even as he ascends to your height and caresses your tenderest
branches that quiver in the sun,
So shall he descend to your roots and shake them in their clinging
to the earth.
Like sheaves of corn he gathers you unto himself.
He threshes you to make you naked.
He sifts you to free you from your husks.
He grinds you to whiteness.

He kneads you until you are pliant;
And then he assigns you to the sacred fire, that you may become
sacred bread for God's sacred feast.
All these things shall love do unto you that you may know the
secrets of your heart, and in that knowledge become a fragment of
Life's heart.
But if in your fear you would seek only love's peace and love's
pleasure,
Then it is better for you that you cover your nakedness and pass out
of love's threshing-floor,
Into the seasonless world where you shall laugh, but not all of your
laughter, and weep, but not all of your tears.

The people who have realized the meaning of life have only spoken to those who can understand love, because love is the meaning of life. Very few people have realized that love is your very flame. It is not food that keeps you alive, it is love – which keeps you not only alive, but gives you a life of beauty, truth, silence, and millions of other priceless things.

The world can be divided in two parts: the world where everything has a price and the world where price is meaningless. Where prices are no longer relevant, values arise. Prices are for things, for dead things.

Life does not recognize that which is dead. But man goes on missing such a simple truth. He even tries to purchase love; otherwise there would not have been prostitutes. And it is not only a question of prostitutes. What are your marriages? – a permanent institution of prostitution.

Remember, unless you enter into the world of values where no money, no power, no respectability is of any help, you cannot enter into authentic life. And the flavor of that life is love.

Because man is so much accustomed to purchasing everything, he forgets that the very effort to purchase something that cannot be purchased is a murder. A husband demands love from his wife because he has purchased her, and the same is true about the wife. But they are unaware that they are assassinating each other. They do not know the moment price enters into love, love dies.

Love is very delicate, very sacred. In all of our relationships we are trying to reduce the other person to a thing. A "wife" is a thing. If you have any intelligence, let her remain just a woman. A "husband" is no longer alive. Allow him to remain in freedom because only in freedom can love flower.

But man, in his utter stupidity, has destroyed everything that is valuable. You even try to purchase God. How deep is your blindness? People who can afford it – remember the word *afford* – have temples in their houses. Statues can be purchased, but whatever you do with those statues is sheer nonsense; a purchased statue can never become a living god. And not only do they purchase the statue, they also purchase a priest to do the worship.

I have seen priests running from one house to another house because they have to worship in at least ten or twelve temples; only then can they feed themselves. And the people who are purchasing even prayer, worship, think they are doing great virtuous acts. These are the sinners!

Your life will not have any flowers if it does not have something which is priceless. Do you have something in your life which is priceless?

People are selling even their lives. What are your soldiers? – and their number must be millions all around the earth. They have sold themselves. Their only function is to kill and be killed. But as far as I can see that is not important; they have killed themselves the day they sold themselves. They may be still breathing, but just to breathe is not life. Trees breathe, vegetables breathe. Cabbages and cauliflowers breathe, but they are not alive and they know nothing of love. They have prices attached to them. Perhaps cabbages are cheaper, cauliflowers a little costly – because cauliflowers are nothing but cabbages with university degrees. But don't do this to any human being.

And if you cannot purchase a thing, you cannot possess it either. In your deep sleep you even possess your children, without ever becoming aware that the very possession – "This is *my* child" – is a murder. Children come through you, but they belong to the universe. You are just a passage. But you make every effort that your child should have your family name, your religion, your political ideology. He should be just an obedient object.

When I was a student in the university the government of India passed a resolution, that unless you participated in training for the army, your postgraduate degree could not be given to you. It was compulsory. I approached the vice-chancellor and I said, "I would love to remain without any postgraduate degree. I am not willing to participate in a training which is nothing but a very psychological process of destroying your consciousness, your life, and reducing you to just a number."

In the army, when somebody dies, on the notice board it is declared, "Number sixteen has fallen." When you read that "Number sixteen has fallen," nothing happens to your heart because number sixteen has no wife, no children, no old mother, no old father to be taken care of. Numbers don't produce children. This is a strategy. But if you see a name, you will suddenly feel sad. What will happen to the children, to the wife, to the old mother, to the old father who was just living to see his son coming back home? But he does not know that his son no longer exists. He has become number sixteen. Number sixteen can be replaced and *will* be replaced. Somebody else will become number sixteen.

You cannot replace a living human being – but a dead number? But it is not only the soldiers: if you look at yourself, in many ways you have allowed the crowd around you to make you a number. Even the people who say that they love you simply want to possess you, to exploit you. You are an object of their longings, of their desires.

Love is not available in the marketplace. For love, you will have to understand that existence is not a dead existence. It is full of light, overflowing with love, but to experience that love you have to be attuned with the world of values.

Almustafa did not answer some people. Perhaps they were not worth answering. They have lost their souls: somebody has become a governor, somebody has become a president. Presidents and governors and prime ministers don't have any souls; otherwise it would be impossible for a man like Joseph Stalin to kill one million Russians. And these were not capitalists – Russia has never been rich – these were poor people, but they did not want to be possessed by anyone and they were rebelling against slavery. First the czars were killing them for centuries, but Stalin outdid all the czars.

But sometimes I think perhaps he killed only dead people. Adolf Hitler killed six million human beings – but perhaps it is not right to condemn him, because these six million people had lost their souls long before. Somebody had become a husband, somebody had become a wife, somebody had become a father, somebody had become a mother...

In the world of nature, a woman is just a woman – not a lady. A lady is a woman who is living a posthumous life. In nature, there are authentic men – raw, rooted in the earth – but you will not find your gentlemen. They are the hypocrites who have died long ago and are now just breathing, eating, dragging themselves from the cradle to the grave. If they were really alive, they would have known the secret that exists between birth and death.

Almustafa simply refused to answer those people – who may have been knowledgeable, who may have been rich, but their questions were phony. Their questions were American.

I must remind you: the word *phony* comes from America. It is derived from *telephone*. When you are talking to someone on the telephone, have you observed the change? The voice is not the same, the tone is not the same, and no one knows whether on the other side there is another American or a ghost.

I have heard...

A great psychoanalyst was treating a super-rich billionaire. Although his fee was beyond the capacity of millions of people, for the super-rich it was nothing.

The rich man continued. A year passed, and he would lie down on the psychoanalyst's couch and would say all kinds of absurd things, which are in your heads too; it is another thing that you keep them within, but in psychoanalysis you have to bring them out.

The psychoanalyst was getting bored but he could not get rid of the super-rich man because he was getting so much money from him. Finally, he found an American solution to it: he said to the rich man, "I have so many other patients and sometimes your session takes three hours, four hours, five hours. You have time, you have money. I have a humble suggestion to make. I will keep a tape recorder which will listen to you. My four or five hours will be saved and at night when I have time, I can listen to the tape."

The rich man said, "Great!"

The next day when the psychoanalyst was entering his office, he saw the rich man coming out. He said, "So quick? Are you finished?"

He said, "No, I have also brought my tape recorder. My tape recorder is talking to your tape recorder. Why should I waste five hours? When tape recorders can do it, what is the need of me coming every day?"

This is how, slowly, slowly, man becomes more and more mechanical. He says things, he lives a life, but it is all like a robot.

Dale Carnegie, one of America's most famous philosophers – he would not be recognized as a philosopher anywhere else except in America – but his book, *How to Win Friends and Influence People* has sold second only to the Bible. And it is full of crap. He suggests that every husband, at least three or four times a day, should say to his wife, "Darling, I love you so much, I cannot live without you. I cannot conceive of myself without you." Whether you mean it or not does not matter.

Do you see the phoniness? If you are in love, it is so difficult to say "I love you," because words fall short. And to repeat three, four times a mechanical routine... You don't mean anything, you are just a gramophone record. Perhaps the needle on the record is stuck: "Darling, I love you." And the darling also answers, and deep inside both hate each other: "This is the woman who has destroyed my freedom." "This is the man who has put me into a prison."

Love is the highest value. That's why Jesus could say, "God is love." But his statement is two thousand years old. It needs some refinement, it needs to be made up-to-date. God is not love.

I say unto you: love is God. And there is a vast difference between the two, although the same words are used. If God is love, it simply means that is only one of the qualities of God. He may have many other qualities: he may be wise, he may be just, fair, he may be forgiveness...

But when you say "Love is God," the statement is totally different. Then godliness itself becomes a quality of those who know how to love. Then there is no need to believe in God – because it is only a hypothesis. And it is up to you what to make of the hypothesis.

The Jewish God in the Old Testament says, "I am a very angry God, I'm very jealous. I am not nice! Remember, I am not your uncle! I cannot tolerate another God." The Mohammedans have inherited the Jewish conception of God. That's why they have been destroying statues and temples, beautiful pieces of art: because there is only one God and one holy book and one messenger, Mohammed. This is a fascist attitude, ugly, inhuman. What is the problem if there are millions of gods? The world will be far richer. Why are you stuck with one God?

Judaism, Christianity, Mohammedanism, all such religions which believe in one God believe in dictatorship, not in democracy. What is the problem?

Gautam Buddha is perhaps the first democratic religious person, who says that every man is a potential god and, finally, all are going to blossom into godhood. This has a beauty.

Almustafa did not answer those people. Instead he cried, wept, tears came to his eyes because their questions were phony. They were asking simply to show others that they were knowledgeable. You know perfectly well the distinction between a knowledgeable question and an authentic quest. When you want to exhibit your knowledge, there is no quest in your heart: you are asking to show that you are not ignorant.

In fact, before asking the question, you already know the answer – not by your own experience, but borrowed.

A great philosopher in Gautam Buddha's time came to see him. He brought his five hundred disciples with him. Buddha never refused anybody. Even at the last moment when he was dying, he asked if anybody had a question because "Now, I am going, my ship has arrived. And I don't want it to be said by future generations that Gautam Buddha was alive and yet he did not answer an authentic question."

Buddha asked the philosopher, "Is it your question or a quest?"

The philosopher said, "What is the difference?"

Buddha said, "The difference is unbridgeable, of the earth and the sky. A quest is a thirst. A question is a mind game. If you have a quest, I am ready to answer. But if it is only a question, don't waste my time."

Almustafa did not answer those people amongst whom he had lived for twelve years and who had never asked anything. But when Almitra, the woman who had recognized him on the first day in the city of Orphalese asked, he answered. And he answered with such beauty, with such poetry, with such truth. Perhaps nobody else has answered that way – not even a person like Krishna, who answered his disciple Arjuna, questions after questions...

Perhaps Arjuna's questions are authentic, but Krishna's answers are not. He is not concerned with the quest. His whole concern is political – to somehow persuade Arjuna to participate in the war. So he goes on answering in different ways which contradict each other and finally, when he finds that his answers are not convincing Arjuna, he resorts to the last thing which any dictator is bound to fall upon.

Finally, he says, "It is God's will that you should participate in the war." It is strange that God is speaking to him and not to Arjuna directly. If I had been in the place of Arjuna, I would have said, "It may be God's will for *you* – fight! But as far as I am concerned, it is God's will not to fight, but to renounce this whole nonsense of destroying and killing people and move deeper into the Himalayas to meditate."

But he became afraid. If it is God's will, he has to fight. He forgot a simple thing: why does God always need mediators? Why can't he speak directly?

In fact, there is no God. These mediators are the most cunning people in the world. In the name of God, they are forcing their own ideas. Because they cannot force through their arguments, their final strategy is to bring God in.

I have always wondered: is God your real question? – any-body's? It is philosophical, intellectual, hypothetical – but what would you do if you met God? And what is the point of meeting God? No, that is not the real quest of man.

Almitra does not ask Almustafa, "Speak to us of God." No, she asks:

Speak to us of Love.

It has to be noted that only a woman can ask about love. Man wants to know God or to become God. These are power trips. Love is not a power trip. Love is the only experience in which you become humble, simple, innocent.

And what does Almustafa say? Meditate over it. Each single word is of immense significance:

And he raised his head and looked upon the people...

Before answering, you have to look into the hearts of people to see whether there is any stirring, whether love is their quest. Almitra has asked a very fundamental question; the *most* fundamental question. But what about the people, the crowd who have gathered there?

...and there fell a stillness upon them.

A great silence, because they were simple people; and as Almustafa looked around into their eyes, into their faces, there was a great silence. Those simple people really wanted to know what Almitra had asked about. Perhaps they were not articulate enough to ask the question; Almitra had become their voice. She represented their hearts. Seeing that:

And with a great voice he said:
When love beckons to you, follow him...

Do not doubt, do not be skeptical, because love is beckoning you toward something you have not known. Although you have the seed... But the seed has not known its own flower. *When love beckons to you,* you are blessed, *follow him...*

Though his ways are hard and steep.

Love is not just a bed of roses.

And when his wings enfold you yield to him...

Do not resist, do not be reluctant, do not go half-hearted. Don't be wishy-washy.

Though the sword hidden among his pinions may wound you.

And love certainly wounds people, but that wound is something like a surgical operation. You are carrying so much hate – that hate has to be destroyed. For a time you may feel a wound, an empty space where hate used to be.

And when he speaks to you believe in him...

He's not saying believe in what he speaks, remember. He is saying when he speaks, believe in *him.* There is a very subtle distinction. If I am speaking to you, you can believe in what I am speaking – that will be from the head, and that is not going to help in any way because tomorrow somebody may speak against it, with better arguments, with more logic. Then you will shift.

Almustafa is saying *believe in him,* not what he is saying. This is a tremendously potential statement: Whenever a master speaks, do not be bothered too much about his words. If the words can only help you to believe in the authenticity of the master, they have done their work. When you believe in a person, it is from the heart. It is not an argument. When you believe in words, it is from the head. It is just an argument.

Life is not an argument, and love is not an argument. It is a meeting of two hearts, two beings – two bodies become one. That is what Almustafa is saying:

Though his voice may shatter your dreams...

It is going to shatter your dreams. It is going to shatter your sleep, it is going to shatter *you.* Just believing in words will not shatter anything in you. On the contrary, you will become more knowledgeable, your ego more decorated.

Though his voice may shatter your dreams as the north wind lays waste the garden.
For even as love crowns you so shall he crucify you.

Never before has anybody spoken, in a single sentence, the whole alchemy of man's transformation. Love will crown you, but it will also crucify you. It will crucify you as you have been, your past, and it will crown you as you should be, your future. Love is both a crowning and a crucifixion. Because of this, millions of people miss the glory of love. The crucifixion makes them afraid – and what is the point of being crowned if you are going to be crucified?

But you are not one, you are many. The real you will be crowned and the false personalities will be crucified, and these processes are going to happen simultaneously. On the one hand, death; on the other hand, resurrection.

Even as he is for your growth so is he for your pruning.

You have grown so many ugly things in your life. They have to be pruned – and that pruning is not against your growth. In fact, those ugly things that you have gathered around yourself – jealousy, domination, continuous effort to have the upper hand – will not allow you to experience love.

When I read that sentence I remembered my gardener, Mukta. She goes on pruning my trees. I know what she is doing *is* right, because unless you prune them they will not grow. But, whenever she sees me – once in awhile I come out of the room – she hides her garden scissors. Mukta, from today there is no need to hide, but only prune that which is against the growth of the tree; don't prune according to your idea of how the tree should be. Let the tree be itself, give it freedom, and if a gardener cannot love his own trees, who is going to love? Prune whenever you see that it will help to bring more foliage, more growth, more leaves, more flowers.

I am not against pruning. Six years before I had told her not to do it because there was a beautiful creeper on the back fence of my garden. But it was wild, and Mukta is a Greek... Just to prune it she named it "the monster." This is one of the strategies of the human mind – whenever you want to destroy something, first, you give it a name, and that becomes the argument for you. That poor creeper was not a monster. Yes, it was wild, but to be wild is not to be a monster – *I* am wild, but do you think you can prune me? I have not even cut a single hair off my beard, they are the originals. You all have unoriginal beards. I have never cut a single hair off my mustache. Just a few days ago there was a question, "Osho, everything you say reaches to my heart but one question remains – how do you manage to eat?"

I can understand his question – an unpruned mustache has almost covered my lips. That's why I never come to eat with you. I always eat alone just to protect my original hair; it is a little difficult...

Even as he ascends to your height and caresses your tenderest branches that quiver in the sun...

You will enjoy it when love reaches to your heights with tenderness, caressing your branches dancing in the wind and in the sun and in the rain. But that is only the half of it.

So shall he descend to your roots and shake them in their clinging to the earth.

And you cannot choose one and avoid the other. Love is a solid phenomenon, it cannot be cut into fragments. Just as your heights need to be showered by love, your roots which are clinging to the earth have to be shaken, because every clinging is an imprisonment. Love would like to give you wings to fly – and with a clinging mind, with attachment, it is impossible to fly in the open sky. Just to cling to the earth, you have grown great roots going deep down so that nobody can shake you. It is out of fear, but fear is just the opposite pole of freedom.

Don't cling to anything, not even to the person you love. Clinging will destroy the very love to which you were clinging. Don't become a bondage.

I have heard...

A great freedom fighter had gone for a holiday in the hills. On the way, he stopped for a night's rest in a small *caravansarai*. The owner of the *sarai* had a beautiful parrot, and in accordance with his beauty, he had made a golden cage studded with diamonds. The owner also loved freedom, so he had taught the parrot only one word: "Freedom." The whole day long the parrot used to call, "Freedom! Freedom!" and his voice would echo and re-echo in the valleys.

This freedom fighter thought, "This is strange. I know the owner; he's my friend. I know his love for freedom – that's why he has taught his parrot only one word, *freedom*. But this is very contradictory. If he loves freedom, let the parrot be free. Even the golden cage studded with diamonds is not freedom." So he waited. In the middle of the night the parrot again shouted, "Freedom! Freedom!" And the voice of the parrot echoed far and wide in the silences around.

The man came out. It was night and the owner was asleep. No one was around. He opened the door of the cage and waited: such a freedom-loving parrot, seeing the door open, will immediately fly into the sky. But instead of flying into the sky, the parrot clung hard to his golden cage.

But the freedom fighter was not a man to be defeated by a parrot. He put his hand inside the cage and pulled the parrot out. While he was pulling the parrot out, the parrot was hitting his hand, scratching his hand and still shouting, "Freedom! Freedom!" His whole hand was full of blood, but he threw the parrot into the open sky on a full-moon night. The hand was wounded, but he felt deeply contented that the parrot was free.

He went to sleep. In the morning he was awakened again by the same voice: "Freedom!" He said, "My God, he has come back!" He looked out. The door was still open and the parrot was inside.

Love will caress you. But it will also go deep down to your roots and shake them to make you free.

It is something to be remembered: most of us go on living in a contradiction. On the one hand we want freedom; on the other hand we go on clinging to something. Freedom is a risk. In the cage the parrot is safe, secure. In freedom, although he gains the whole existence, the whole sky, he loses the safety and the security.

But freedom is such a value, anything can be sacrificed for it. And love needs absolute freedom to grow. Only then can you make the whole sky your home. People afraid of insecurity, unsafety, choose just the word *love* but never experience it.

If you want to experience love, you will have to risk everything and all – all your clingings, all your future safeties. But instead of sacrificing clingings and safeties and securities, man in his deep sleep has sacrificed love and saved security.

That is what your marriage is – love is sacrificed. There is security; of course in marriage there is security, there is safety. There is a guarantee that tomorrow, too, the wife will be available to you, the husband will be taking care of you. But what about love? Then *love* becomes an empty word.

Be aware of empty words, and particularly words like *love*, which are higher than God – God is only a quality of love. Don't go on carrying an empty container with no content in it. This is your misery, the misery of the whole humanity. Nobody loves.

Love is risky. I teach you to take all the risks, because even a single moment of love is equal to the whole eternity. And a life without love may be immortal, but will be just a graveyard. Nothing will blossom. You will be secure – but what will you do with your security?

Like sheaves of corn he gathers you unto himself.

But if you are clinging to something else how can existence, or God, or love, gather you unto himself?

He threshes you to make you naked...

...because you are covered with so many fake personalities. Your face is not your original face. There are so many masks.

He threshes you to make you naked.
He sifts you to free you from your husks.
He grinds you to whiteness.

The word *whiteness* has to be understood – it is not a color. You can have the whole rainbow, but you will miss two colors which you have become accustomed to – black and white. And why have all the mystics condemned the black and praised the white?

White is not a color but *all* the colors. If you mix all the colors of the rainbow, whiteness arises. So whiteness is basically a great synthesis of all the colors of life. And if you remove all the colors, then there is blackness. Blackness is negativity, blackness is no. Blackness is death.

Whiteness is positivity, whiteness is yes, whiteness is godliness. Whiteness is love.

He kneads you until you are pliant;
And then he assigns you to his sacred fire, that you may become
sacred bread for God's sacred feast.

All the religions of the world had been teaching people to fast. Almustafa is talking about a feast. Against all the religions, I am in agreement with Almustafa. Life is not a fasting, it is a continuous feast – a celebration, a festival of lights.

Love transforms your life into a festival of lights.

And unless your life becomes a feast and a festival, remember: you have not done the thing you have come for on this earth.

All these things shall love do unto you that you may know the
secrets of your heart, and in that knowledge become a fragment of
Life's heart.
But if in your fear you would seek only love's peace and love's
pleasure,
Then it is better for you that you cover your nakedness and pass out

of love's threshing-floor...

People want love but they don't want to be prepared for all the threshing, the fire that they have to pass through. They think love is just pleasure. It is not. Love is far more: it is blissfulness, it is the ultimate benediction. But you will have to drop fear.

The man who is full of fear will never know the sweet taste of love. And if you have not known love, you have not known anything: all your knowledge is useless, all your treasures are useless. All your respectabilities are useless.

Almustafa says rightly:

Then...cover your nakedness and pass out of love's threshing-floor,
Into the seasonless world where you shall laugh, but not all of your
laughter, and weep, but not all of your tears.

You will never know anything in its wholeness, in its totality. You will laugh but your laughter will be superficial. You will weep but your tears will be crocodile tears. Your life will always remain just a potentiality, it will never become a reality. And you will live your life in sleep – unconscious.

2

LOVE
love possesses not

Love gives naught but itself and takes naught but from itself.
Love possesses not nor would it be possessed;
For love is sufficient unto love.
When you love you should not say, "God is in my heart," but
rather, "I am in the heart of God."
And think not you can direct the course of love, for love, if it finds
you worthy, directs your course.
Love has no other desire but to fulfill itself.
But if you love and must needs have desires, let these be your
desires:
To melt and be like a running brook that sings its melody to the
night.
To know the pain of too much tenderness.
To be wounded by your own understanding of love;
And to bleed willingly and joyfully.
To wake at dawn with a winged heart and give thanks for another
day of loving;
To rest at the noon hour and meditate love's ecstasy;
To return home at eventide with gratitude;
And then to sleep with a prayer for the beloved in your heart

and a song of praise upon your lips.

Almustafa has the deepest insight into love that anyone has ever shown. These are not the words of a philosopher, these are the experiences of a mystic.

Almustafa is just a name. It is Kahlil Gibran who is speaking through him – and for a special reason. He could have spoken directly in his own name; there was no need for Almustafa to be a medium. But Kahlil Gibran does not want to create a religion, although whatever he has said is the fundamental religiousness. To avoid it, because in the name of religion so much inhumanity to human beings has been done, so much bloodshed...

Millions of people have been killed. Thousands have been burned alive. The moment any religion becomes organized and crystallized it becomes a danger to all that is valuable in life. Then it is no longer the path to godliness, it becomes an excuse for war.

Kahlil Gibran keeps himself hiding behind Almustafa so people don't start worshipping him, so people don't continue the ugly past. Rather than saying directly what he wants to say, he has created a device: Almustafa. Because of Almustafa, his book is not counted as a holy book – although it is one of the most holy books in the world. Compared to it, all other holy books will appear unholy.

He created Almustafa so that his book would be taken as fiction, as poetry. This is his compassion, and this is his greatness. You can look in all the holy scriptures; you will not find words so alive that they go directly like arrows into your heart. And you will find much that is inhuman, unworthy of remaining in those holy scriptures. But man is so blind – just the small fiction of Almustafa, and people have forgotten a simple fact: that these truths cannot be asserted unless you have experienced them, unless they are your own.

Kahlil Gibran has prepared the ground for me. He has sown the seeds in unknown fields, in *unremembered seasons.*

I am here in the right time for the harvest. You are my harvest. You are the fruits and the flowers. Talking on Kahlil Gibran is just to remind you about your seeds. And also, something more important...

There is an ancient story in the land of Kahlil Gibran – one of the most beautiful lands on the earth, Lebanon. It is famous only for two things – Kahlil Gibran, and thousands-of-years-old cedar trees which are still trying to reach toward the stars.

Kahlil Gibran was also doing that. The cedars of Lebanon have not succeeded yet, but Kahlil Gibran has succeeded. Perhaps one day those cedars will also reach the stars.

In all the paintings of one of the most important Dutch painters, Vincent van Gogh – perhaps the most important as far as insight, understanding is concerned – the trees always go beyond the stars; the stars are left behind. He was thought mad by his contemporaries. He was asked again and again: "Where have you seen trees growing above the faraway stars?"

Vincent van Gogh said, "I have not seen them, but sitting by the side of the trees I have heard their longings. And I paint the flower even before the seed has been sown."

All his stars are strange: he has painted them as spirals. Even the painters laughed at him: "You must be insane. Stars are not spirals."

He said, "What can I do? Not only in my dreams, but even in my wakefulness my heart always feels that they are spirals." He could not sell a single painting in his whole life – who would purchase such paintings? And he painted them with his blood, with his very life.

From his younger brother, he used to get just enough money every week so that he could eat two meals a day for seven days. He used to fast three days of the week so he could purchase paints, canvasses. No other painter has painted with such longing, with such deep love.

He lived just to paint; he died when he was thirty-three. And just a few months ago, physicists have come to the conclusion that stars *are* spirals – one hundred years afterward.

The poet has certainly some unknown short-cut to knowing things. He cannot prove it. He is not a scientist, he is not a logician. But the contemporaries are thousands of years behind. It is very rare to find an individual who is authentically contemporary. Rajiv Gandhi, the prime minister of India, won the election on a single slogan: "I want India to enter the twenty-first century." And not a single man in this vast country of nine hundred million people asked him whether the country has yet reached the twentieth century! People are living in thousands-of-years-old superstitions, in ideologies which have no relevance to truth. And they are not willing to come out of their darkness.

I would like my people to be not only of this century or of the twenty-first century; I would like my people to be the people of the whole future. When you can be masters of the whole future, why unnecessarily remain beggars?

Listen to these words, because these are not words, these are living flames. It is pure fire. If it cannot consume you, you have not heard it:

Love gives naught but itself and takes naught but from itself.

Such a tremendous statement, which will always remain fresh; I cannot conceive of any time in the future when this statement will become out of date. If you can understand it, if you can live it, the whole future also becomes yours. It can open the doors of the unknown reality that awaits you.

Love gives naught but itself... You also give when you are in love – flowers, ice cream, *bhelpuri*. But this is not love, this is bargaining, business.

In a small school, the teacher had been insisting on the greatness of Jesus for almost an hour to the students. The school belonged to a church; it was an international school.

After an hour, she asked, "Can anyone say who is the greatest man in history?"

A little boy, an American, said, "Abraham Lincoln."

The teacher could not believe it. For one hour she had been hammering into their heads that Jesus Christ is the highest peak human consciousness has ever achieved, and this idiot says "Abraham Lincoln!"

She said, "You are not wrong, but not right either. Sit down."

Another girl stood up to answer the same question and she said, "Winston Churchill."

The teacher said, "My God!" But because the school was in England and Winston Churchill was the prime minister, she could not say, "You are not right." She said, "You are very close to the truth."

And then a very small boy started waving his hand – and this was strange, because this boy had never done such a thing. He was a very silent individual.

The teacher said, "What is your answer?"

He said, "There is no question; everybody knows Jesus Christ is the greatest man in the world."

The teacher was shocked even more, because the boy was a Jew. But there was a shield waiting – whoever gives the right answer is going to win the shield. The little boy, carrying the big shield, was followed by the teacher and caught outside the school. The teacher said, "Listen, are you not a Jew?"

He said, "Of course I am. What is the problem? Why are you fol-lowing me?"

She said, "Being a Jew – and you declare Jesus Christ to be the greatest man in the world?"

He laughed. He said, "Ah, yes. In the deepest core of my heart, I know that Moses is the greatest man in the world. But business is business."

Love is not business, but man has reduced love into business. Love gives only itself, because there is nothing higher to give. Can you think of anything greater? Anything more valuable?

Love gives naught but itself and takes naught but from itself – that is even more significant to understand. Love knows only giving; even the idea of getting something in return does not arise. But this is the miracle of existence: if you give love, love returns your own love a thousandfold back to you.

There is no need to be a beggar. Love makes you an emperor. It gives itself, and strangely enough, finds that the same love has become a thousandfold and has returned from all directions. The more you give it the more you have it.

Humanity looks so poor because we have forgotten the cosmic law. Instead of giving, love has become a beggar, it is continuously asking. The wife is asking, "Give me love, I am your wife." The hus-band is saying, "Give me love." Everyone is asking, "Give me love." Who is going to give? – all are beggars.

You should come near an emperor like me, who gives and goes on giving because it is an inexhaustible source. And the more I have loved people, the more I was surprised: my love has increased and I can give more.

I have heard a story…

A man's dog died. He had been very loving toward the dog, and the dog was rare – a beautiful piece of art. It was not just an ordinary dog; generations of crossbreeding had created it. The man was very sad. He went to the same pet shop where he had purchased the first dog, and said that he wanted something better; otherwise he would not be able to forget his old dog.

The owner said, "Don't be worried. I have a very rare dog – and very cheap." He showed him the dog and certainly, the man had never seen such a beautiful dog with such a philosophical face, with such loving eyes, with such a beautiful body.

He said, "I am ready to pay anything."

But the owner said, "He's not very costly, he's the cheapest dog I have. There are more costly dogs if you want."

The man went around and he was surprised: those costly dogs were nothing compared to that cheap dog. He asked the owner: "I'm puzzled and confused. Why are you selling that dog so cheaply?"

The owner said, "You don't understand. First purchase it, and then you will understand."

So he purchased the dog – at such a cheap price! You could not even get a vagabond dog from the street at that price.

Puzzled, he went home. In the morning he looked and the dog had disappeared. He said, "My God, where has the dog gone? The house was locked and I am alone."

He rushed back to the shop and the dog was there, sitting in his place. The owner said, "Have you understood why he is the cheapest dog? He always comes back. He has been sold a thousand times but he is so obedient... You can have him," he said, "but what is the point if he comes back, and has been sold a thousand times?"

When I read the story I could remember only one thing in my experience – because I don't have a dog, although dogs come once in awhile. But I know about love. It is not only cheap, it has no price at all.

To be loving costs nothing, and yet it always comes back a thousandfold. You go on becoming richer and richer. It is a strange economics of existence.

Love gives naught but itself and takes naught but from itself.
Love possesses not nor would it be possessed.

The moment you possess anything you have killed it. And millions are the people in the world who have killed their love with their own hands. They should look at their hands: they are covered with the blood of their own love. And now they are miserable; they never wanted to kill it, there was no intention to kill it, but in their unconsciousness they started possessing. If they loved someone, they wanted to possess that person totally. Husbands are possessing their wives, wives are possessing their husbands, parents are possessing their children. Teachers are trying in every possible way to possess their students. Politicians are trying to possess countries. Religions are trying to possess millions of people and their lives. They are all murderers, because the moment you try to possess you have killed.

Life thrives only in freedom. If you love, you will give more and more freedom to your beloved. And love never allows anyone to possess it, because love is your very soul. If you allow somebody to possess it, you have committed suicide.

So love is either murdered or commits suicide. People are simply walking corpses with begging bowls searching for love, for warmth, for tenderness. And they are not going to find it because they have created a stupid society, they have created a mad world.

The basis of everybody going neurotic or psychotic is simple: their souls are not nourished. Love is very nourishment. You can have all the wealth of the world, if you don't have love, you are the poorest man – unnecessarily burdened with wealth, palaces, empires.

But one who loves, one who has known the secret of love – not to possess and not to be possessed – is really born again. He has become, in the true sense, alive. He will have all the beautiful experiences of life, all the great ecstasies of existence.

If love grows in your heart, you are pregnant with godliness. It is godliness growing within you. Slowly, slowly you will disappear and there will only be pure godliness. It is felt: those who have been close to Gautam Buddha or Mahavira have felt it. It is a strange story that neither Mahavira believes in God nor Buddha believes in God. People think that they are atheists, but no, absolutely no. They don't believe in God because they *themselves* are God.

You believe in God because your God is somewhere high beyond the sky; you are just a creature, creeping on the earth. Why should a Buddha believe in God? He's within him, he himself has become the temple of godliness. So although they denied the existence of God, the reason for the denial was not the same as the reason of an atheist.

The atheist denies God because God cannot be proved logically. The atheist should deny love too, because love also cannot be proved logically.

I have known many atheists and I have asked them only one question: "Have you ever fallen in love?"

And they were surprised. They said, "Why are you changing the subject? We were talking about God."

I said, "I am not changing the subject, I am *coming to* the subject. Have you ever fallen in love?"

They said, "Yes, we have loved."

"Then," I said, "think once again. Can you prove scientifically, rationally, logically, that love exists?"

They said, "We cannot."

"Then," I said, "stop denying God, because you have been denying God for the same reasons."

Only a man like Gautam Buddha has the right to deny God, because he has found him. And he has found him not somewhere else, but in himself. Now, God is not an object but his own subjectivity.

And it is strange that these two persons, Gautam Buddha and Mahavira, are the only people in the whole world who have preached nonviolence. *Nonviolence* is their word for *love*. They avoided the word *love* because love has got into wrong company. You go to a prostitute and you say, "I love you." Love has fallen into the gutter. That's why they had to find something virgin, pure. But it means love: *nonviolence*.

And at the same time I must remind you that the people who have believed in God in the sky have not been nonviolent. Mohammed is not nonviolent; neither is Moses, nor is Jesus.

In twenty centuries, Christians have killed so many people that it is impossible to count them. Mohammedans have been killing continuously for fourteen centuries, and the people who are Mohammedans are not those who are converted because of the truth; they are converted because they are cowards. Mohammedanism came to people with a sword in one hand and the Holy Koran in another: "You can choose. There is no need of any argument, the sword is the argument." Those who had some guts died rather than choosing out of fear.

Love cannot arise out of fear. The Christians have changed the tactics because the times have changed, but the story is the same:

the Holy Bible in one hand and a loaf of bread in another: "You can choose." Have you seen anybody being converted to Christianity because of its higher values, greater truth, deeper insights? Have you seen anybody who is rich, cultured, educated being converted to Christianity? No, it needs beggars, it needs orphans, because *they* need food. They are hungry. They are not hungry for truth; they are hungry for bread, they are hungry for a shelter, they are hungry for clothes. Is this conversion?

The Christian church of America got annoyed with me for the simple reason that the well-educated, talented, young generation was coming to me. And my hands are empty; there is neither a sword nor bread nor a Holy Koran nor a Holy Bible.

I can only give you my love, because I know it is going to come back.

Christians became annoyed. They were not annoyed with Vivekananda because Vivekananda was being political. He was telling them, "It is all the same: Christianity, Hinduism, their teachings are all the same." There was no problem with him. They were not afraid of Ramateertha...

Why should they have been so annoyed with me? For almost one year, my sannyasins in Italy – which is the citadel of Catholic Christianity – have been trying to get just a three-week tourist visa for me, and the pope goes on interfering with the government. Just today I received the message that now it has become a burning question in Italy that the government does not say no. If they say no, then my sannyasins are going to the court. And they cannot say yes, because the pope, and the votes...

Finally, a political party of radical revolutionaries saw the whole game: "For one year continuously! You should answer either yes or no. But you always go on saying 'Tomorrow,' and tomorrow never comes." Now the radical revolutionary party has insisted to the prime minister of Italy, "Either give the visa or deny it."

If the pope can enter India, then who are you to prevent me? And when the pope came to India I welcomed him, and I condemned the people who were throwing stones at him and were protesting that he should go back. I condemned those people, the Hindu chauvinists. Those were signs of weakness: if the pope is coming, invite him, welcome him for a discussion. You have your *shankaracharyas* – have open-forum discussions all over the country. And if he is right, let this country be Christian, because the question is not whether Hindu or Christian, the question is to be always with the truth.

I have been continually challenging the pope – I am ready to come to the Vatican, his own city, amongst his own people. I am ready to discuss nothing else but Catholic Christianity. And my condition is simple: if you can defeat me, I will become a Catholic Christian, but if you are defeated, then you have to become a sannyasin! And the Vatican has to become my headquarters.

But such impotent people... They will not say anything, and they go on pressuring the prime minister: "Votes... If this man is allowed, then Catholic votes will not be given to you." Now, the whole country is Catholic, and you will not find politicians who have any spine, they are spineless creatures.

Love possesses not nor would it be possessed;
For love is sufficient unto love.
When you love you should not say, "God is in my heart..."

...because that can become your ego. Hence, Almustafa says:

...but rather, "I am in the heart of God."

He has improved upon the first statement, but the second statement, although better, can still be improved. My suggestion is that you should say, "Love is and I am not."

And think not you can direct the course of love, for love, if it finds you worthy, directs your course.

Relax and trust into love. And allow love to take you. Just as every river goes to the ocean, every small stream of love arising from your heart goes to the universal, to the ultimate, to existence.

Love has no other desire but to fulfill itself.
But if you love and must needs have desires, let these be your desires...

But if you are not strong enough to surrender totally to love and you have other desires too, then, Almustafa says, at least have *these* desires:

> *To melt and be like a running brook that sings its melody to the night.*
> *To know the pain of too much tenderness.*
> *To be wounded by your own understanding of love;*
> *And to bleed willingly and joyfully.*
> *To wake at dawn with a winged heart and give thanks for another day of loving;*
> *To rest at the noon hour and meditate love's ecstasy;*
> *To return home at eventide with gratitude...*

If you cannot let go totally, then slowly, slowly, step by step, move toward gratitude.

> *And then to sleep with a prayer for the beloved in your heart and a song of praise upon your lips.*

3

MARRIAGE
not the marriage you know

Then Almitra spoke again and said, And what of Marriage,
master?
And he answered saying:
You were born together, and together you shall be for evermore.
You shall be together when the white wings of death scatter your
days.
Aye, you shall be together even in the silent memory of God.
But let there be spaces in your togetherness.
And let the winds of heavens dance between you.
Love one another, but make not a bond of love:
Let it rather be a moving sea between the shores of your souls.
Fill each other's cup but drink not from one cup.
Give one another of your bread but eat not from the same loaf.
Sing and dance together and be joyous, but let each one of you be
alone,
Even as the strings of a lute are alone though they quiver with the
same music.
Give your hearts. But not into each other's keeping.
For only the hand of Life can contain your hearts.
And stand together yet not too near together:

For the pillars of the temple stand apart,
And the oak tree and the cypress grow not in each other's shadow.

Almustafa has spoken of love; the next thing to be considered is marriage, obviously – but not the marriage that you know. Not the marriage that the whole world has followed, because it is not out of love. It is not rooted in love. In fact, on the contrary it is a device of the cunning society, the priests and politicians, to bypass love.

Hence in the old days – and in ancient Eastern countries, even today – the child marriage has existed. Children know nothing of life, they know nothing of marriage. In their innocence, all the cultures and civilizations have found a good opportunity to exploit them. Before love arises in their hearts they are already in bondage.

The existing marriage is not only not of love, it is *against* love. It is so destructive that it is impossible to find anything more destructive of human spirit, human joy, human playfulness, human sense of humor.

In a child marriage, the children who are going to be married are not even asked. Astrologers are asked, palmists are asked, the I Ching is consulted, tarot cards are looked into. The decisive factor is not the lives of the children who are going to be married, the decisive factor is the parents on both sides. Love is not at all a concern. They have their own considerations – the family, the prestige of the family, their respectability in the society, the money that is going to be transferred from the girl's parents to the boy's parents. It is strange that the people who are going to be married, who are going to live a long life ahead of them, are completely excluded. It is a business; everything else is considered.

For example, royal families will only allow their children to marry into another royal family. It is politics – pure politics. Just look at Europe's royal families: they are all connected in some way or other by marriage. It avoids conflicts, it avoids invasion – and it makes them stronger. When four or five royal families are connected through their children, they have five times more power. Although it is absolutely against physiology, against the findings of medical science, still it continues, as if royal blood has some more special quality to it than the blood of a commoner. Turiya is here. Her husband was also one of my most intimate sannyasins, Vimalkirti. He was the great-grandson of the German emperor – although the empire is gone, royalty remains.

Vimalkirti was a rebellious spirit. He married out of love: Turiya, a commoner. The whole family was against it – not just his own family but many families in Europe, royal families, because it was against their tradition. And naturally, because they're all connected, Vimalkirti became almost an outcast.

If the empire had still been there, Vimalkirti would have been the emperor of Germany. His mother is the daughter of the Queen of Greece. She is also the sister of England's Queen Elizabeth's husband, Prince Philip. She must have other sisters, other brothers, who have entered into other royal families. They were all against it, they tried hard to stop Vimalkirti from marrying Turiya. But he was a man of integrity and intelligence. He could not understand the superstition. Nobody, no expert, if given few samples of blood can find out which is the royal blood. Blood is blood.

And when Vimalkirti and Turiya came here, that was really outrageous – that the great-grandson of the German emperor, the oldest royal family in Europe, should become a sannyasin and be a bodyguard of a beggar like me, who has nothing of his own. They were so furious that when the Queen of Greece died – and she had become the Queen Mother because she had so many children; almost all the royal families had become connected through her children – her last words were, "Somehow bring Vimalkirti, Turiya and their daughter back from that dangerous man."

But Vimalkirti died – and he died because of this stupid idea of royal families marrying. Then you are really marrying your sisters, your brothers – they are all closely connected. And the closer the connection, the more dangerous; this is the finding of modern science, medicine, physiology, chemistry. Marriages should be between people who are as far away as possible, then children are healthier, more intelligent, more beautiful. Otherwise, certain diseases go round and round in twelve or fifteen families.

When Vimalkirti died we thought it must have been an accident, because he was exercising and he suddenly fell and became unconscious. Every effort was made. In the best hospital... Zareen is here, my sannyasin; Vimalkirti was being treated under her husband, Dr. Modi's care. But all the doctors were convinced: "We could go on keeping him alive with artificial breathing but he's really dead. It is a brain hemorrhage, nothing can be done." After the fourth day, they insisted that they had other patients, and only one emergency room for people who are in a coma. "And Vimalkirti is dead. The moment you remove the artificial breathing, you will see – he is a corpse."

But I insisted that they at least let his mother and father, his brothers arrive. They were coming. The mother and the brother came, and then finally the doctor said, "It is becoming ridiculous." And the moment the artificial breathing was turned off, it was a corpse.

The father came late – and these are the royal people – an old man, who could have been the emperor of Germany. He was not concerned with the death, the possible death of his son, the future of his son's wife, the future of their child. He had gone for a holiday with his girlfriend. And he's just a postmaster, but royal blood, even in a postmaster...

We gave Vimalkirti the best celebration. Perhaps he would not have got that much love, such a beautiful celebration, even if he had been the emperor of Germany. Still the mother, and later on the father who came, were angry at me. Their whole anger against Vimalkirti turned toward me. They were consulting legal experts about how they could sue me in court for the death of their son. They had to stop that, because they would have given me a chance to prove to the whole world that this nonsense of royal marriages should be banned.

They stopped suing me because Vimalkirti had died from a disease that he had inherited. After just a few days, his uncle died in the same way – suddenly fell unconscious, brain hemorrhage, and finished. And later on, I came to know that their grandfather had also died in the same way. For no reason, no disease – just from nowhere the brain hemorrhage, and the man is gone.

They stopped suing me, seeing the situation that I would bring into court: your father was not my sannyasin, Vimalkirti's uncle was not my sannyasin. Rather than suing me, take care of yourself because you will be dying in the same way, it is only a question of time. The disease is inherited.

And all the royal families of Europe have inherited diseases. Just think: not a single man from these royal families has shown any intelligence, any genius. What is the reason? They should be the most intelligent people in the world but they are the most retarded. It is simply a scientific fact that marriage should not happen when you are closely related.

If you are a Hindu, never marry a Hindu; a Mohammedan is better, a Christian is better. If you are a Jew, find a Hindu. And don't be worried because these are also are very close, deep down in the past. Right now you see them as separate – just as you see the branches of a big tree separate, and then the small branches are even more separate. But as you go deeper, you find a trunk – they are all coming from the same source.

My vision is: if man wants to become superman then find out – are there people on Mars or on some other planet? Marriage between those and the people of the earth will create the superman. His life will be long, his health will be superb. His intelligence will be the highest.

But parents have been deciding and asking idiots about decisions; astrologers – what have stars to do with you? You live on such a small planet that stars may not be even aware of your planet. And they are far away; some stars are so far away that they will never know that any planet like earth has ever existed.

Light rays have tremendous speed – ultimate speed. When there was no earth – because the earth is only four billion years old; four billion years ago, from thousands of stars, rays started moving. The rays were not travelling to reach the earth, it was just the natural radiation of the stars. But they are so far away. Although the speed of their rays is ultimate, there is no higher speed than that: a ray travels one hundred and eighty-six thousand miles per second. Just think of one minute; you will have to make the number sixty times more. Think of the whole day; you will have to make that number twenty-four times sixty more. Think of the whole year! You will have to make that number three hundred and sixty-five times more.

We have no idea – because miles cannot be the right measure; otherwise you will have to write a whole book! Thousands and thousands of zeros, just to tell about the nearest star. The nearest star sends its rays in four years, so where you see it, remember, it is no longer there. It used to be there four years ago. So at night you are seeing an absolute illusion, no star is where you are seeing it. Perhaps one thousand years ago, one million years ago, four million years ago it used to be there. Meanwhile, it may have traveled millions of miles.

And there are stars farther away. Their rays have not reached the earth yet, and perhaps by the time their rays reach the earth, there may be no earth at all.

[Here the electricity fails, taking with it the audio and video recording. After a few moments of silence, Osho resumes speaking.]

In this vast universe, the earth is so small, negligible. Even compared with the sun, it is very small: the sun is thousands of times bigger than the earth. And our sun itself is a mediocre fellow. There are suns thousands of times bigger, which you see as stars. They look small because they are so far away. Such a small earth, and we have divided it into hundreds of small pieces. And made man a foreigner to other men.

Just see the stupidity of the whole thing: just before 1947, the people living in Pakistan were not foreigners; now they are foreigners. The people living in Bangladesh were not foreigners; now they are foreigners.

Politicians cannot live without creating conflict, fight, war. For that, all these divisions are needed, and each division tries to hold its people within its fold. That is the reason you cannot marry a Mohammedan woman or a Hindu man. Your society will be bloodthirsty – a man or a woman is going out of the fold, there is one vote less. Truth does not count; neither does man's well-being. All that counts is power. And power is the need of the most inferior people.

A man cannot eat power, cannot drink power – why is there so much struggle? Why does he want to be on top, in control of everything? He suffers from an inferiority complex. He knows deep down he's nobody, and he's afraid that if he does not prove himself to be somebody special, extraordinary, then people are going to discover his nobodiness, his ordinariness.

A real person of superiority has no lust for power. The lust for power arises out of inner poverty, the lust for money out of inner poverty. The parents are not interested in their children's joyful life, they are interested in them being rich, well-connected, because those connections, those contacts are helpful in rising higher on the ladder of power.

So, for thousands of years, marriage has been one of the ugliest things invented by power-lusty people.

Almustafa is not talking about the marriage you know. He's not talking even about the love marriage – that is a recent development in developed countries. Child marriage has disappeared and people are marrying when they fall in love. But love they know not; the mystery of love is absolutely unknown to them. In fact, they are calling something else love. They are calling lust, love – your so-called love marriages are nothing but blind lust.

Love is never blind – because there exists the confusion, and you don't make the demarcation: people have started talking about "blind love." Love gives you the clearest vision, fresh eyes. Lust is certainly blind because it is biological, it has nothing to do with your spirituality.

Then Almitra spoke again and said, And what of Marriage, master?

For the first time, she's addressing Almustafa as *master*, because the time of separation is coming close. And whatever he has said about love only a master can say – one who knows, one who knows from his own experience.

And he answered saying: You were born together...

Don't misunderstand this statement. He's not saying that every man is born with a possible wife somewhere. He's saying something totally different. He's saying: *You were born together.* You were born together in love because you became new, you became fresh, you became young, you became a song, you became a dance that you have never been.

...and together you shall be for evermore.

If you are born out of love, if your togetherness is not out of lust, your love is going to deepen every day. Lust lessens everything, because biology is not interested in whether you remain together or not. Its interest is reproduction; for that, love is not needed. You can go on producing children without any love.

I have been observing all kinds of animals. I have lived in forests, in mountains, and I was always puzzled: whenever they are making love they look very sad. I have never seen animals making love joyfully; it is as if some unknown force is pressuring them to do it. It is not out of their own choice; it is not their freedom but their bondage. That makes them sad.

The same I have observed in man. Have you seen a husband

and wife on the road? You may not know if they are husband and wife, but if they are both sad you can be certain they are.

I was traveling from Delhi to Srinagar. In my air-conditioned compartment there were only two seats, and one was reserved for me. A couple came, a beautiful woman and a young, beautiful man. Both could not be accommodated in that small coupe, so he left the woman and he went into another compartment. But he was coming at every station, bringing sweets, fruits, flowers.

I was watching the whole scene; I am just a watcher. I asked the woman, "How long have you been married?"

She said, "It must have been seven years."

I said, "Don't lie to me! You can deceive anybody else, but you cannot deceive me. You are not married."

She was shocked. From a stranger, who had not spoken, who had simply been watching. She said, "How did you come to know?"

I said, "There is nothing in it, it is simple. If he were your husband then, once he had disappeared, if he had come back at the station where you were going to get off you would be fortunate!"

She said, "You don't know me, I don't know you. But what you are saying is right. He's my lover. He's my husband's friend."

I said, "Then everything is okay."

What goes wrong between husbands and wives, even after a love marriage? It is not love, and everybody has accepted it as if he knows what love is. It is pure lust. Soon you are fed up with each other. Biology has tricked you for reproduction and soon there is nothing new – the same face, the same geography, the same topography. How many times have you explored it? The whole world is sad because of marriage, and the world still remains unaware of the cause.

Love is one of the most mysterious phenomena. About that love, Almustafa is speaking.

You were born together, in the moment love arose in you. That was your real birth. *And together you shall be for evermore,* because it is not lust. You cannot be bored, because it is not lust.

Once you have reproduced children, biology has left you and you find it strange living with a stranger. The woman is not known to you, the man is not known to you. All that you are doing is quarreling, nagging, harassing each other. This is not love.

Love is the flowering of meditation. Meditation brings many treasures; perhaps love is the greatest roseflower that grows on the bush of meditation.

You shall be together when the white wings of death scatter your days.
Aye, you shall be together even in the silent memory of God. But let there be spaces...

Remember these statements: *...let there be spaces in your togetherness.*

Be together but do not try to dominate, do not try to possess and do not destroy the individuality of the other. And that is being done everywhere.

Why should the woman take the name of the man? She has her own name, she has her own individuality. Just think: the man taking the name of the woman – no man would be ready for it. But you have destroyed the woman because she is fragile, delicate, humble.

Why should the woman go to the man's house? Why shouldn't the man go to the woman's house? Once in a while it happens that the man goes because the woman he has married, he has married on the condition that he will be going to live in her house, because the father of the woman has no son who is going to look after his properties, possessions. But have you seen? – whenever a man goes to live in his wife's house, he's condemned by everybody. He's laughed at, as if he has lost his manliness. But nobody laughs at the woman.

In fact, man is more capable of going to the woman's house. She is more fragile. To take her from the garden where she has grown, to uproot her, is the beginning of destruction. She can never be an individual in the man's house. She's going to be just a slave, uprooted, unconnected with anyone. She's just a servant. And that's the way she has been treated all over the world.

My own suggestion is, the moment a man and woman decide to live together, they should have their own house. Nobody should go to anybody else's house, because whoever goes to anybody else's house is going to be a slave. And slaves cannot be joyous. They have lost their integrity, their individuality. They have sold themselves.

But when you live together, *let there be spaces*. The husband comes home late; there is no need, no necessity for the wife to inquire where he has been, why he's late. He has his own space, he's a free individual. Two free individuals are living together and nobody encroaches on each others' spaces. If the wife comes late, there is no need to ask "Where have you been?" Who are you? – she has her own space, her own freedom.

But this is happening every day, in every home. They are fighting over small matters, but deep down the question is that they are not ready to allow the other to have his own space.

Likings are different. Your husband may like something, you may not like it. That does not mean that it is the beginning of a fight; that because you are husband and wife, your likings should also be the same. And all these questions: every husband returning home has going on in his mind, "What is she going to ask? How am I going to answer?" And the woman knows what she's going to ask and what he's going to answer, and all those answers are fake, fictitious. He's cheating her.

What kind of love is this that is always suspicious, always afraid of jealousies? If the wife sees you with some other woman – just laughing, talking – that's enough to destroy your whole night. You will repent: this is too much just for a little laughter. If the husband sees the wife with another man and she seems to be more joyous, more happy, this is enough to create a turmoil.

People are unaware that they don't know what love is. Love never suspects, love is never jealous. Love never interferes in the other's freedom. Love never imposes on the other. Love gives freedom, and the freedom is possible only if there is space in your togetherness.

This is the beauty of Kahlil of Gibran – tremendous insight. Love should be happy to see that his woman is happy with someone, because love wants his woman to be happy. Love wants the husband to be joyous. If he's just talking to some woman and feels joyous the wife should be happy, there is no question of quarrel. They are together to make their lives happier, but just the opposite goes on happening. It seems as if wives and husbands are together just to make each other's lives miserable, ruined. The reason is they don't understand even the meaning of love.

But let there be spaces in your togetherness. It is not contradictory. The more space you give to each other, the more you are together. The more you allow freedom to each other, the more intimate you are. Not intimate enemies, but intimate friends.

And let the winds of the heaven dance between you.

It is a fundamental law of existence that being together too much, leaving no space for freedom, destroys the flower of love. You have crushed it, you have not allowed it space to grow.

Just recently, scientists have discovered about animals that they have a territorial imperative. You must have seen dogs pissing on this pillar, pissing on that pillar – you think it is useless? It is not. They are drawing the boundary: "This is my territory." The smell of their urine will prevent another dog from entering. If another dog comes just close to the boundary, the dog whose territory it is will not take any note. But just one step more and there is going to be a fight.

All animals in the wild do the same. Even a lion, if you don't cross his boundary, is not going to attack you – you are a gentleman. But if you cross his boundary, then whoever you are, he's going to kill you.

We have still to discover human beings' territorial imperative. You must have felt it, but it has not yet been scientifically established. Going in a local train in a city like Mumbai, the train is so overcrowded; people are all standing, very few have found seats. But watch the people who are standing – although they are very close, they are trying in every way not to touch each other.

As the world becomes more overcrowded, more and more people are going insane, committing suicide, murders, for the simple reason that they don't have any space for themselves. At least lovers should be sensitive, that the wife needs her own space just as you need your own space.

One of my most-loved books is by Rabindranath Tagore, *Akhari Kavita, The Last Poem.* It is not a book of poetries, it is a novel – but a very strange novel, very insightful.

A young woman and a man fall in love and, as it happens, immediately want to get married. The woman says, "Only on one condition." She is very cultured, very sophisticated, very rich.

The man said, "Any condition is acceptable, but I cannot live without you."

She said, "First listen to the condition; then think it over. It is not an ordinary condition. The condition is that we will not live in the same house. I have a vast land, a beautiful lake surrounded by beautiful trees and gardens and lawns. I will make you a house on the other side, just opposite where I live."

He said, "Then what is the point of marriage?"

She said, "Marriage is not destroying each other. I am giving you your space, I have my own space. Once in a while, walking in the garden we may meet. Once in a while, boating in the lake we may meet – accidentally. Or sometimes I can invite you to have tea with me, or you can invite me."

The man said, "This idea is simply absurd."

The woman said, "Then forget all about marriage. This is the only right idea – only then can our love go on growing, because we always remain fresh and new. We never take each other for granted. I have every right to refuse your invitation just as you have every right to refuse my invitation; in no way are our freedoms disturbed. Between these two freedoms grows the beautiful phenomenon of love."

Of course the man could not understand, and dropped the idea. But Rabindranath has the same insight as Kahlil Gibran...and they were writing at almost the same time.

If this is possible, to have both space *and* togetherness, then...

The winds of heaven dance between you.
Love one another, but make not a bond of love...

It should be a free gift, given or taken, but there should be no demand. Otherwise, very soon you are together but you are as apart as faraway stars. No understanding bridges you; you have not left space even for a bridge.

Let it rather be a moving sea between the shores of your souls.

Don't make it something static. Don't make it a routine. *Let it rather be a moving sea between the shores of your souls.* If freedom and love together can be yours, you don't need anything more. You have got it – that for which life is given to you.

Fill each other's cup but drink not from one cup.

He's just trying to make you understand how these apparently contradictory things – space and togetherness – are possible: *Fill each other's cup but drink not from one cup.* The distinction is very subtle but very beautiful.

> *Give one another of your bread but eat not from the same loaf.*
> *Sing and dance together and be joyous, but let each one of you be alone...*

Don't reduce the other in any way.

> *Even as the strings of a lute are alone though they quiver with the same music.*

The strings of the lute are alone, but they quiver with the same music. The separation, the space, is in the individuality of the strings. And the meeting and melting and merging is in the music. That music is love.

> *Give your hearts. But not into each other's keeping.*

Giving is great. Love gives unconditionally, but it does not give its heart *into each other's keeping.*

> *For only the hand of Life can contain your hearts.*
> *And stand together yet not too near together...*

One has to be very, very alert. Stand together but without destroying the other. Not too much together – leave spaces.

> *For the pillars of the temple stand apart...*

Just look at these pillars. They stand apart but still they support the same roof. There is space, individuality, and yet there is a merger and meeting because they are supporting the same roof.

> *And the oak tree and the cypress grow not in each other's shadow.*

This much space is needed – that the other is not under your shadow. Otherwise, it will not grow.

Why are people who are in love constantly angry, sad? – because their own growth is not happening. One of the two has covered the whole sky and has not left even a little space for the sun, for the wind, for the rain to reach the other. It is not love, it is ownership, possessiveness.

Love would like you to grow at the same rate, to the same height, so that you dance together in the sun, in the wind, in the rain.

Your togetherness should be an art.

Love is the greatest art in existence.

4

CHILDREN
life's longing for itself

And a woman who held a babe against her bosom said, speak to us of Children.
And he said:
Your children are not your children.
They are the sons and daughters of Life's longing for itself.
They come through you but not from you,
And though they are with you yet they belong not to you.
You may give them your love but not your thoughts,
For they have their own thoughts.
You may house their bodies but not their souls,
For their souls dwell in the house of tomorrow, which you cannot visit, not even in your dreams.
You may strive to be like them, but seek not to make them like you.
For life goes not backward nor tarries with yesterday.
You are the bows from which your children as living arrows are sent forth.
The Archer sees the mark upon the path of the infinite, and He bends you with his might that His arrows may go swift and far.
Let your bending in the Archer's hand be for gladness;

For even as He loves the arrow that flies, so He loves also the bow that is stable.

I t is almost impossible to find a book comparable to Kahlil Gibran's *The Prophet,* for the simple reason that it has a tremendous inner consistency: first he talks about love, then he talks about marriage and now he's going to talk about children. This is how the river of life flows – from love to marriage to children.

And a woman who held a babe against her bosom said, speak to us of Children.

Before I start my meditations on Kahlil Gibran, one more thing has to be noted – that all three of these questions have come from women. Men also ask questions but they are always abstract, about God – who the hell is this guy? Just an invention of man's mind, and nothing much, it is not an authentic question – about heaven and hell and about thousands of other things, but all abstract. They don't touch your life at all. You can live perfectly well without a God. In fact, you *are* living perfectly well – whether God is or not makes no difference to you.

I have seen the theists and I have seen the atheists. If you talk to them, their ideas are just diametrically opposite to each other. But if you look at their lives they are the same. You can see their real problems by observing their lives: they are about love, they are about marriage, they are about children. But in their books, in their philosophies, they are talking about things which do not matter at all.

Do you see the difference? The woman is more realistic, more pragmatic, more earthbound. She has roots. Her inquiries are not just games and puzzles about empty words. And, for centuries, the woman has not been allowed even to ask. It is because of this that people's minds are full of all kinds of garbage and their lives are empty. They do not know anything about the real problems that have to be encountered every moment, from the cradle to the grave.

A great philosopher of India, a contemporary man, Dr. Ranade was the most respected and the most learned scholar, logician. He was a professor of philosophy at the University of Allahabad. In his days, the department of philosophy at the University of Allahabad had become the most prominent department of philosophy in India, and India has almost one thousand universities.

I saw him just a few days before he died. He was very old, retired, but still people used to come from far and wide – not only from this country but from all over the world – to ask questions, to inquire.

I was sitting with him. He said to me: "What are your questions?"

I said, "I know not."

"Then why have you come to me?"

I said, "Just to see you and to see the people who are continually coming to you from morning till night."

I watched him for almost six hours, and all the people who came had come with abstract questions: "Does God exist? Is the soul a reality? Is there life beyond death?" And he was answering them.

After six hours I said to him: "You are old, and I'm young. It doesn't look right for me to say, but perhaps we may not see each other again, forgive me if it hurts you: you have wasted your whole life. In these six hours I have seen in what way you have wasted it. I have not heard a single question or a single answer that *really* concerns life. And these people have come from faraway places and you have lived a long life, but as far as I am concerned... Don't feel that I'm not respectful to you, I am saying this because I *am* respectful. Whatever small time you have left, don't waste it. At least in the evening of your life, inquire into something which is authentic."

He was shocked, because nobody had ever told him this. But he was an honest man. He said, "I am old, and you *are* young, but you are right."

The real question is not whether life exists after death. The real question is whether you are alive before death.

The real question is not whether God is love, just, fair, compassionate. The real question is, do *you* know what love is? Do *you* know what justice is? Do *you* know what compassion is? Have *you* lived and tasted all these treasures of existence?

The real question is not whether the soul exists or not. The real question is, have you ever entered into yourself to see whether there is any inner reality, or are you just a container without any content?

Kahlil Gibran is not a philosopher of the abstract. The people who are so interested in the abstract are really escaping from the real problems of life. They are cowards, not philosophers. But these cowards are dominating the whole world's thinking.

All these questions are coming from women. And there was a great crowd of people – there were learned people, there were priests, there were philosophers. But when they asked, Almustafa – who represents Kahlil Gibran – did not answer them. The questioner may be an idiot; that does not mean you have to answer his stupid questions.

But the moment Almitra came out of the temple, Almustafa started answering the way perhaps nobody else has ever answered.

If you ask a great philosopher like Martin Heidegger or Jean-Paul Sartre or Emmanuel Kant about children, they will laugh. They will say, "We are philosophers and we are not interested in trivia. Children? – is this a philosophical question? Marriage? – is this a philosophical question?" Just look in the contents of the great philosophical treatises of the world and you will not find love, marriage, children, there.

But I say to you, all those great treatises are just escapes from the realities of life. Emmanuel Kant is interested in the existence of God but is unable to love anyone. He was not a friend to anyone. These are small things, and these people are great philosophers. But I repeat again: they are cowards.

A woman asked Emmanuel Kant... She had waited long, because it is not the way of the woman's heart to take the initiative, it looks ungraceful. But life is short. You cannot wait too long. And youth is even shorter, and beauty is just a flower that blossoms in the morning and is withered by the evening. Finally the woman – against feminine nature, against herself – said to Emmanuel Kant: "I love you. Do you love me? Just a small yes and I can wait for my whole life."

But Emmanuel Kant could not say yes. He said, "First I have to think about it." It took him three years to consult all the books of different races, countries, of different centuries, to collect data about marriage – for and against. And he was very puzzled because they were all balanced. There were reasons in favor of marriage and there were reasons against marriage and their weight was equal.

His servant – he lived his whole life with a servant – had been watching those three years. He said, "Listen to me: I am not a philosopher, I am a poor man, your servant, and it is none of my business, but there is a limit. I have been repressing my temptation to say something to you and today I have decided to say it.

"When you went to university, I looked into your notes for and against marriage. They are equal; hence you cannot take any decision. Just one thing I want to say to you: that is, that you have not experienced love. And all these arguments are impotent, they cannot give you any experience. My humble suggestion is, when both sides are equally weighty and decision is difficult, always decide for yes because that is opening a door to experience. No will close the door to experience."

Emmanuel Kant could not believe that this thought had never occurred to him. He rushed, knocked on the woman's door. An old man came out. He introduced himself: "I am Emmanuel Kant and perhaps you are the father of the woman. I have come to say yes."

The old man said, "It is too late. She is already married and she has two children. Go and knock on some other door."

But he was such a coward, he could not gather courage to approach another woman. All his great philosophy... And the same is the case with all other great philosophers. But nobody has looked into the psychology: why are they interested in absurd, meaningless problems and not in the real problems of life? Real problems need courage.

The world has known not a single woman who was a great philosopher. And how can a woman be a great philosopher? She wants to know: *speak to us of Children*, about marriage, about love. A woman has a certain authenticity, for the simple reason that all her interest is in the small matters of life, the intimate matters of life – matters which she has to face moment to moment.

Alas, it has been a great loss. The world is full of stupid philosophies, rooted in fear and cowardliness. It would help humanity immensely if the woman was listened to, if her questions were respected and answered not just through the head but through the heart.

A man's question has no need of the heart. In what way is God connected with your heart? Or life beyond death? These are all thoughts in the head.

Remember this: Kahlil Gibran's *The Prophet* opens a totally new dimension to philosophy, gives credit and respect to small things of life – because life is made of small things and if you cannot solve them, forget all about great problems. How can you solve them? You are simply asking about them because you don't want even to be aware of the real and the pragmatic problems of life.

And he said...

Listen very carefully, because very few statements exist in the whole literature of the world which have such beauty, such truth, such sincerity:

Your children are not your children.

A child is not a thing. You cannot possess a child. To say, "This is *my* child," is to assert your ignorance.

Life can never be possessed. You can have it in open hands, but the moment your hands become closed fists, life has escaped out of them. Almost all the parents of the world have destroyed their children because they have claimed ownership. To own a child? You cannot create life, how can you own it? It is a gift from the abundance of existence. Be grateful that you have been chosen to be a vehicle.

The child has come through you but that does not mean he belongs to you. You have been nothing but a passage. If parents had remembered this small and simple truth, the world would have been a totally different place.

They are the sons and daughters of Life's longing for itself.

It is the eternal life, flowing through mountains, through forests, through plains. The child that has come through you has been coming through many other people before you. He has eternity behind him and eternity ahead of him. He had been in many houses, in many cities, in many strange places. In those millions of vehicles, you are also one. Be humble and be respectful to the child. No society in the world, up to now, has been respectful to the children. All respect is for the elders, all respect is for the old, almost dead. All respect is for the graveyards; no respect for the cradles.

And the child is the purest life – uncontaminated.

Almustafa is right when he says:

They are the sons and daughters of Life's longing for itself.
They come through you but not from you...

They are coming from the very beginning.

And though they are with you yet they belong not to you.

These small statements have tremendous implications if you
understand that the child is: *Life's longing for itself.* Then the child
is closer to the very source of life than the old man. The old man is
closer to death. But strange – death has been worshipped, respected,
and life has been crushed, destroyed in every possible way.

If you know they come from you but they do not belong to you,
then no parent is going to impose his religion, his politics, his ideas on
the innocent child. He comes as a tabula rasa – nothing is written
on him – and the parents are in such a hurry to make him a Christian,
to make him a Hindu, to make him a Buddhist.

I remember my own childhood. My parents naturally wanted me
to go with them when they went to the temple, to the religion they
belonged to, but I have been a little bit crazy from the very beginning.

I told them, "It is your religion, it is your temple. You should have
a little more patience. Give me time. I will find my own religion, my
own temple."

They said, "What kind of nonsense are you talking? Every child
belongs to the religion he is born into."

I said, "Every other child may belong, may not belong – that is
their business. As far as I am concerned, I do not belong to any religion. I have not even searched for it. Allow me and help me to stand
on my own feet. Don't cripple me. Don't destroy me. If there is truth,
I will find it. But it cannot be borrowed – you cannot give it to me."

They were obviously not happy. I never wrote with my name,
the name of my religion... It was good that I entered school a little
later than other children, because my mother's father had only one
daughter, my mother. And he lived in a faraway village where
people had not seen the railway train, a car, a bus, because there
was no road.

He asked my father: "I feel very lonely since you have taken my
daughter as your wife. Let your first child be with us. We feel very
empty, all the joy of our life has disappeared." And my mother was

only seven years old when she was married. That's how things used to be in India – and still are in the villages.

They said, "Our daughter was our joy, she was our song. She was our life. And she is so young, she may not be able to take enough care of the child. Let the child grow with us, and of course later on you can take him back. And you will have many more children."

It was such a great blessing to me. My father's mother died when he got married; he was only ten years old. When I was born, he must have been twenty years old and my mother, seventeen years old. And they themselves were at a loss how to raise a child. So it was a good opportunity. I was raised by my maternal grandfather and grandmother. But there was no school – I was so fortunate all the way – there was no temple, there was no priest. I grew almost like a wild child, and I have remained a wild child still.

My maternal grandfather died when I was seven years old. This was old enough to have one's own ideas, so when I came back to my parents, we were strangers. I had never known my mother as my mother. I had known my grandmother.

The first seven years are the most important in life, because they are the foundation. So when my father took me to the school and filled out the form in which he was required to write to what religion I belonged, I stopped him.

I said, "Write down 'as yet, he belongs to no religion. He will search, he will try to find.'"

My father said, "But that will look very strange."

I said, "No, truth, however strange it is, is never really strange. And a lie, however familiar, is never familiar. It does not exist at all."

And it remained a problem with me as I moved from one school to another, from college to the university, everywhere. It is taken for granted that everybody is born into a religion. And this is absolute stupidity. How can one be born into a religion? You may be born to a father who is a doctor – that does not mean that you become a doctor because you are born as the child of a doctor. Your father and mother both may be doctors – that too, does not make any difference. If you want to be a doctor, you will have to go through the whole education, examinations; only then could you become a doctor.

For ordinary things, you know perfectly well that a child is not born a doctor, is not born a professor, is not born a scientist. How can he be born as a mystic?

Filling out forms was always a problem. The clerk would say, "The form has to be filled completely. You have left out one thing."

I said, "I have to leave it out, because I don't know my religion yet."

And I was sent again and again to the principals: "What to do with this boy? He says he has not found his religion yet but the requirement is that the form should be filled out completely. Nothing should be left empty."

I said, "You can reject my form, you can refuse me admission to your institution, but I cannot lie. I don't have a religion."

They persuaded me. Lovingly, they would say, "It is just a form. Your father must have a religion."

I said, "This form concerns me, not my father. As far as my father is concerned, I have put his religion with his name. But I don't have any religion."

They had to accept it. I said, "In fact, you should withdraw this type of form in which religion is required."

Even when I graduated from university... The education minister was well known to me because he had been a vice-chancellor and I had been to his university many times for debating competitions. I had taken all their shields and their cups, so he was well acquainted with me.

It was a requirement that you had to win a shield continuously for three years and then it became yours. Otherwise, you would keep it for one year and return it the next year when again there would be a debate. But I went on winning continuously. He said, "You are a strange person. These shields, these cups had been with us since the university was established fifty years ago, because nobody was able to win continuously for three years. And now we are in trouble: every year we have to purchase a new shield, a new cup and we know that if you appear again..."

He had become the education minister so I went directly to him. I said, "I have passed my postgraduate examination, I have topped the whole university, and I want to be appointed immediately to any university you feel is right."

He said, "This is not the way. You first fill out the application form." And again, the same problem: "What is your religion?"

I said, "What has religion to do with my qualifications as a teacher? I don't have any religion. And if you refuse me, I am going to have my first press conference."

He said, "Don't do any such thing. Just write anything, any religion. Write it in such a way that nobody can read it. But the form has to be filled out."

I said, "I cannot do that."

Since my first entry into school, that line on my forms has remained empty. It is still empty. I have found religiousness but I have not found any religion. And I am immensely happy that nobody tried to force upon me their idea, their God, their concept of existence.

Every child has the birthright not to be tortured and conditioned by his parents, because everybody's most fundamental right is the search, the seeking, the pilgrimage.

And though they are with you yet they belong not to you.
You may give them your love but not your thoughts...

But just the opposite is being done. Do you remember your parents? Were they interested in giving you their love, unconditionally? Or they were interested in using their love to contaminate your mind with their religion, with their political ideology, with their nationality. Otherwise, how is it that humanity is so divided? Who is the criminal behind it? Why should there be so many nations? Why should there be so many religions?

Humanity is one. Truth is one. But people have not been allowed to search for their own original face. They have been given masks, and people live their whole lives believing that this is their original face.

How do you know you are Christian? You have never been with Christ. You were not given the choice, the opportunity to choose whether you would like to be in love with Christ or Gautam Buddha or Mahavira or Lao Tzu or Zarathustra.

Your religion is your bondage. It is your imprisonment. Your Christianity, your Hinduism, your Mohammedanism, your Jainism are all chains which you cannot see, because they are not binding your body, they are binding your very soul. Any man who has accepted ideologies from others has sold himself. He's a slave, although it is being said from every pulpit in every country that slavery has disappeared.

I say it is not true. Yes, slavery has changed its form; it has become more dangerous. If you handcuff me, still my spirit is free; if you chain my feet, still my spirit is free. You can destroy my body, still my spirit is free. But to pollute your mind with Hinduism, Buddhism, Mohammedanism, Christianity, is to bind invisible chains around your very spirit. This is the real crime. And all the parents of the world up to now are responsible for it.

You may give your love but not your thoughts,
For they have their own thoughts.

Their thoughts have not yet become mature, they are still in seed form. They are still only potentialities, but given freedom and love they will become realities, they will become actualizations. And when your own thought becomes a reality it brings such joy to your being, such fulfillment, such bliss that you cannot dream about it. You cannot have any notion about it; it is beyond the capacity of your mind to conceive it because it ripens in your heart, it blossoms in your heart.

You may house their bodies but not their souls...

With all good intentions, all parents are murderers of their own children. You see all over the earth only dead people walking, who have lost their souls even before they had any notion of what it is.

For their souls dwell in the house of tomorrow, which you cannot
visit, not even in your dreams.

You belong to the past; your days are over. Parents cannot conceive of the future, and children are not going to live in the past, so don't burden them with your dead scriptures. They will have their own scriptures, they will have their own saints. They will have their own Buddhas, they will have their own Christs. Why should they be burdened with the past? They have an open future.

And if you love your children, you should keep your hands off. Help them to be strong, help them to be able to go on the search for the unknown, but don't give them your ideas; they are absolutely useless to them. Because of them, they will miss their own destiny. You are distracting them.

Just watch small children and see the clarity of their vision.

I have heard...

In a small school, a Christian priest is teaching the children that God created all things, the whole universe, in six days – and on the seventh day he rested.

One small boy stood up and he asked, "What about railway trains?"

The priest was at a loss. Certainly, there is no mention in the New Testament or in the Old Testament that God created railway trains. Another small boy started waving his hand. The teacher said, "You also have a question?"

He said, "No, I want to answer."

He could not believe that he could not find the answer and this small child... He said, "Okay, let us try. What is your answer? This boy is asking, what about railway trains?"

The other boy said, "It is written that God created all creeping things – railways trains are included!"

Small children have an insight and a clarity. As you become older, you start gathering dust. And everybody is giving you advice – advice is the only thing in the world which everybody gives and nobody takes – but this is corrupting the minds of the small children who are dependent on you.

Almustafa is right: ...*house their bodies but not their souls. For their souls dwell in the house of tomorrow.* You belong to the yester-days, they belong to the tomorrows. Give as much love as you can. The present is a meeting point, but also a point of departure. From the present, where you are meeting, you will depart. Every day, the gap between you and your children will become bigger and bigger.

They talk of the generation gap. The generation gap is one of the most beautiful things that has happened in this century. Make every effort to widen it, make it almost unbridgeable. Otherwise you will be carrying corpses all your life.

Gautam Buddha died twenty-five centuries ago. Jesus died two thousand years ago. Is man insane? Why should anybody go on car-rying dead bodies? You are twenty-five centuries ahead. Evolution has not stopped with Gautam Buddha; Gautam Buddha is twenty-five centuries back. But because you are burdened with that dead corpse you cannot create your own buddhas.

If you are absolutely free of the past you will find higher peaks of consciousness – higher than any Christ and higher than any Buddha. We are not falling downward. Our consciousnesses are reaching toward the stars, but it is so difficult to understand such an obvious truth. The past is the greatest barrier to your life.

The police commissioner... Remember, I can forgive him but I cannot forget him. I will go on hammering on his head – even if he's in his grave, my hammer will go on hammering him.

He has asked the ashram in-charge that I should not criticize any religion. What does it mean? It means I should not criticize the past – and the past has been so ugly that it needs all the criticism that one can make so that it can be erased from your minds, and your minds can be made available to the future.

You are pregnant with many Buddhas and many Christs. Why should you go back? But because you are already burdened I have to condemn them and I have to criticize them – although I accept the freedom of everyone to criticize me. But I had never thought that I was going to face such an impotent humanity. It is nothing but impotence that is asking, "Don't criticize any religion."

Mohammedans are marrying four wives. If you criticize it you are criticizing their religion, because in their holy book, the Koran, Mohammed allows them to marry four or more women. I would not criticize it, I would not have talked about it, if Mohammed had given the same right to women too, so that each woman could marry four husbands. Then the man would have been fair. Fortunately, nature knows nothing about Mohammedanism.

And why am I saying "fortunately"? Because one woman is enough to finish you! Four women for every man – then you will see, in every house, a Jesus Christ hanging on a cross!

I have heard that a thief was caught red-handed, stealing, in a house. The magistrate asked, "At what time did you enter the house?"

He said, "Nearabout ten in the night."

The magistrate said, "But what were you doing the whole night? because you were caught early in the morning, six o'clock."

He said, "It is a long and sad story. I just want you to remember: whatever punishment you want, you can give to me. Even crucifixion is acceptable but don't punish me by telling me to marry two women."

The magistrate said, "You seem to be a strange person. The whole night you were in the house. You have not stolen anything, but you have been found in the house and now you are asking that I should not punish you by making you marry two women? No such punishment exists. Don't be worried about that. But what is the whole story?"

He said, "The whole story is, unfortunately: I entered the house; the man has two wives. One wife lives on the ground floor, and the second wife lives on the first floor. And they were both dragging the man to their floors – on the steps, one woman would come and drag the man upward, and the other woman would come and drag him back downward. It was so interesting that I forgot all about my own business, what I had come there for. And anyway, stealing was impossible because the man was crying and the women were screaming... So please, just avoid this punishment!"

Nature produces an equal number of men and women. The concept is against nature, and nobody can prevent me from condemning it, criticizing it. Yes, everybody has the right to answer my criticism. Mohammed himself married nine women. What do you think of women? Are they *things?* Commodities? Cattle? And if it were only that it happened fourteen centuries before, a story, there would be no need to be worried about it. Just in this very century, the Nizam of Hyderabad had five hundred wives – and you want me not to criticize it? But the poor Nizam is nothing compared to the Hindu god, Krishna – he had sixteen thousand wives!

And at least this can be said in favor of the Nizam and Mohammed, that they married women with the consent of their parents. Krishna, whom Hindus think is a god, simply took away any woman who was beautiful. They were almost all women married to other men. They had their children, they had their husbands. They had to look after their own houses, their own families.

This criminal behavior, just because he had the power, the armies... His soldiers would go into anybody's house and drag out the woman he wanted. In this way, he collected sixteen thousand women, a great collector of women. But what about those sixteen thousand families? Their children, their husbands, the old father of the husband, the old mother of the husband? And I am not to criticize any religion.

If you have any answer, I am ready to pay my total attention. And if you can convince me that this kind of behavior is religious, moral, worthy of a man you think is a god, I will accept it. But first you have to prove it. Because you cannot prove it, to hide your impotence you are preventing me, saying that I should not criticize any religion.

The whole past of humanity is my past too, it is *my* inheritance too, and I have every right to criticize my past, my inheritance. Wherever I see something ugly, inhuman, barbarous, I *have* to criticize it as strongly as possible. And those who don't want their religions to be criticized should leave those religions, they are of no worth.

I have never said, in my whole life, that whatever I am saying should not be criticized. In fact I have been inviting people to criticize me, because I know what I am saying has a truth. And if I cannot criticize the past – the ugly past, the rotten past – then how we are going to create a better future?

You have heard the proverb that history repeats. It repeats because of people like this man. If the past is criticized, it will not be repeated again, but if you can go on doing anything in the name of religion... For example, Sikhs are allowed to have a sword because it is their religious thing. Strange – if Sikhs are allowed to have a dangerous weapon that can destroy any life, then what is the guarantee and defense for other people? Either everyone should be allowed or nobody should be allowed. Double standards simply show that it is a political game because you are afraid. The Britishers were afraid; for three hundred years, they allowed Sikhs to carry swords.

But then we can make our own religious ideas – nobody can criticize them. I can make it a point that every sannyasin should have a machine gun. It is our religious right. What is wrong in it? The police commissioner has ordered us that no firearms should be inside this place. He should look at his face in a mirror. Then why are the Sikhs allowed? And I'm not saying that Sikhs should not be allowed, I am simply saying there should be one standard for all human beings. These double standards are ugly, immoral, corrupt.

He has asked that police officers should be allowed in the discourses. Can he ask the same to the Mohammedans, that police officers should be allowed in their prayers, in their sermons, inside their mosques? And if he cannot do that, he cannot do it to us.

He asks that inside this place or outside this place, there should be no "obscene behavior" from the sannyasins. All the scriptures of the Hindus are obscene, and anybody who has any guts, I welcome him: I will show him what is written in his scriptures. In the Holy Bible, there are five hundred pages of absolute obscenity. And still it is the "Holy Bible." You cannot find a more unholy book in the whole world.

One of my friends has collected all the five hundred pages and published a book. No government is going to allow that book entry into their country, it would be banned. But strange – those five hundred pages are verbatim from the Bible. If you are banning anything, the Bible should be banned. But strange... Double standards everywhere.

Parents should not give their thoughts to their children because their thoughts are already out of date. The children will have their own thoughts.

Even trees know better. Every fall, the old leaves drop and disappear into the earth to give a place for the new leaves – greener, younger, juicier. If they go on clinging to their old leaves, there will be no space, no possibility for the new leaves to appear.

Have you ever wondered why, in the contemporary world, people like Buddha, Lao Tzu, Chuang Tzu, Basho, Kabir, Jesus, Zarathustra are not born? What has happened? Is humanity a spent force? No, humanity is more powerful, has more energy than ever. But the past goes on becoming bigger and bigger. Naturally, every day, one day is joined with the yesterdays. And now the past has become almost like a Himalaya on the fragile chest of human beings. This is the reason you don't have such beautiful beings. And if once in a while a man arises, he looks like such a stranger, such an outsider that you cannot tolerate him. You have forgotten the taste of the world when there were thousands of enlightened people all over. Nobody was annoyed. People were full of gratitude.

But today the situation is completely different. All that burden on the mind prevents you from seeing the new. And the new is bound to tell the past, the dead, to get lost.

I have been looking into all the scriptures of all the religions: they are all obscene. Still, no government dares to ban them. And they ask that my people should not behave in any obscene way.

First take care of your own house. First clean your own mind, and if you cannot do it, I am here and my people are here. Come here, we do dry brainwashing! Just one thing is needed – that you should bring your brain with you, because I have heard...

A politician was on the surgery table – in fact, every politician should be there. But this politician was going nuts. Even other nuts started saying to him, "You have crossed the limit!"

So finally, he went to a brain surgeon. They looked into his brain and they said, "My God! This seems to be a politician's brain – everything is wrong."

So they took out the whole brain to clean it. They went into another room, because it would take almost six hours to clean it. While they were cleaning his brain in the other room, two persons came running, shook the politician, who was lying alone in the surgery room. He opened his eyes.

They said, "What are you doing here? You have been chosen to be the prime minister of the country!"

He jumped, rushed out with his friends. When the doctors had cleaned his brain, they came back: the man was missing. They had never done such hard work. They said, "My God, where has he disappeared to – and without a brain!"

They went in search, inquired. Somebody said, "We have seen him with two persons, rushing toward the prime minister's house."

So the surgeons went there and saw him. He had become the prime minister of the country. The surgeons said, "You have forgotten your brain in our surgery!"

He said, "Don't bother, just keep it safe. As long as I'm prime minister, no brain is needed."

Don't give your rotten past as an inheritance to your children. They have their future. Let them grow according to their own potential.

You may strive to be like them...

This is where Kahlil Gibran simply surpasses in his insights:

You may strive to be like them, but seek not to make them like you.

And what does the Bible say? "God made the man in his own

image." Since that time, every father is trying to make his child in his own image. Almustafa is saying just the opposite: *You may strive to be like them,* because they are of the future, and they are innocent. They are closer to existence than you are. For you, there is nothing except death to happen, but to them millions of things are going to happen: love is going to happen, meditation is going to happen, gratefulness is going to happen. Please resist the temptation that your child should be a carbon copy of you. It is possible to make the child a carbon copy of you, but you will have to kill him. That's what I'm saying, that all the parents are killing their children just to make them carbon copies. And the child has the potential to be his own original face.

The original face has beauty, the original face has something of the divine. The original face has charisma. A carbon copy has nothing.

For life goes not backward nor tarries with yesterdays.
You are the bows from which your children as living arrows are sent forth...

...toward the unknown and the unknowable. Don't prevent them. Give them strength, give them love, so they can reach to the farthest star.

You are the bows from which your children as living arrows are sent forth.
The Archer sees the mark upon the path of the infinite, and He bends you with His might that His arrows may go swift and far.

Existence wants you to bend like a bow before your own children because they have to travel far and you have to give them strength.

Let your bending in the Archer's hand be for gladness...

Be glad when your child starts moving away from you, when he starts becoming an individual in his own right. Feel blessed that he is not an obedient idiot. Except idiots, nobody is obedient.

Intelligence is rebellion. Feel blessed and bless the child: that you have given birth to a rebellious spirit. This should be your pride, but this becomes people's anxiety.

Let your bending in the Archer's hand be for gladness;
For even as He loves the arrow that flies, so He loves also the bow
that is stable.

Existence loves you both. You are also children of the same existence.

It is just that your time is over; give place to the fresh arrows and bless them.

5

GIVING
when you give of yourself

Then said a rich man, Speak to us of Giving.
And he answered:
You give but little when you give of your possessions.
It is when you give of yourself that you truly give.
For what are your possessions but things you keep and guard for fear you may need them tomorrow?
And tomorrow, what shall tomorrow bring to the over-prudent dog burying bones in the trackless sand as he follows the pilgrims to the holy city?
And what is fear of need but need itself?
Is not dread of thirst when your well is full, the thirst that is unquenchable?
There are those who give little of the much which they have — and they give it for recognition and their hidden desire makes their gifts unwholesome.
And there are those who have little and give it all.
These are the believers in life and the bounty of life, and their coffer is never empty.
There are those who give with joy, and that joy is their reward.

And there are those who give with pain, and that pain is their baptism.
And there are those who give and know not pain in giving, nor do they seek joy, nor give with mindfulness of virtue;
They give as in yonder valley the myrtle breathes its fragrance into space.
Through the hands of such as these God speaks, and from behind their eyes He smiles upon the earth.
It is well to give when asked, but it is better to give unasked, through understanding;
And to the open-handed the search for one who shall receive is joy greater than giving.
And is there aught you would withhold?
All you have shall some day be given;
Therefore give now, that the season of giving may be yours and not your inheritors'.

Almustafa is entering into the world of man, and particularly the man who is rich. Before I say something about his magnificent statements, a few remarks are absolutely necessary.

Life up to now has been corrupted by ambition. There is no other poison which is more potent than ambition because it kills you and yet keeps you breathing. Ambition turns you into vegetables, and the lure of ambition is given to every child with the mother's milk. From the very first moment his whole life is being based on principles of destructiveness. Nothing destroys more than ambitiousness.

You have all been told – by parents, by teachers, by priests, by neighbors, by all these so-called well-wishers – that you have to become somebody special, important, powerful. And money gives more power than anything else, because even the politicians are commodities in the market: you can purchase them.

In fact, every politician is sold into the hands of the super-rich. But the super-rich person is the poorest on the earth. He has succeeded in being important, in being powerful, but he has lost his soul. Inside, there is just emptiness and darkness.

Why does it happen? What is the mechanism of its happening? Ambition is a ladder, and you always see somebody ahead of you. It is competitive. Your whole mind is continuously thinking of ways and means, right or wrong, to reach higher than others. And if you are cunning enough you may succeed, but in the world of ambition, success is the ultimate failure. A man becomes alert and aware about the failure only when he has reached the last rung of the ladder. He has wasted his whole life in search of being higher than others, holier than others, richer than others. And now his desire is fulfilled.

Cursed are those people who reach the final stage of their ambition. Their ambition has been their dream day and night – and it is not easy, because everybody else is also trying for the same success. But by the time you have reached the last rung of the ladder you are in for a great surprise and a shock, because there is no longer anywhere to go and your whole training in life has been just to compete, to fight. It is no ordinary competition, it is cutthroat; it does not matter how many people you destroy. Your eyes are fixed on a faraway fulfillment.

You have heard the saying – it must have been created by the idiots – that "Nothing succeeds like success." It is not the saying of a man who has really succeeded, because, I say to you, nothing fails like success. You have reached the goal but your whole life has slipped by. There was no time for anything – not even to breathe properly, not even to smile, not even to love. What kind of life have you lived? It was like a robot, mechanical, and now that you have arrived at the desired goal there is tremendous frustration in your being, because nothing is there.

But very few have been courageous enough to say that it is a strategy of the society to keep people away from living. The whole of society is against life, against love, against songs, against dances. Trees are far happier, flowers are more joyous. Those who are sensitive can even hear the sermons in the stones. But those are not the people who are after some goal, because a goal is always tomorrow. Meanwhile, you are miserable. Who knows whether you are going to succeed or not? You have staked your whole life on success, but even if you have all the wealth of the world you cannot eat it. It cannot be a nourishment to your life and your spirit. On the contrary, it has made you a rich beggar, surrounded by riches but at the very center of your being there is just a begging bowl.

I am reminded of a small story, very ancient. A king, a great king has come out of the palace just to have a little walk in his beautiful, vast garden. As he stepped out, he faced a beggar with a begging bowl. And the beggar said, "I am fortunate to find you directly. Otherwise... I have been waiting for months for an appointment, but who cares to give an appointment to a beggar?"

The king said, "What do you want?"

He said, "My longing is not for much. Just this small begging bowl – fill it with anything that you think, as a great king, is worthy of you. Don't think about my worth, I am a worthless beggar. Think about yourself – fill it with something that you think you are worthy of."

The king had never seen such a beggar: who is not asking because he is hungry, because he is thirsty, because he has nothing to live on. On the contrary, he is saying, "Think about yourself. Your gift should have the signature of a great king, anything will do."

This was a great challenge, and the king called his prime minister. Before he could say anything to the prime minister, the beggar said, "But remember one thing, one condition: the bowl has to be filled completely."

The king said, "Don't be worried. I have so much, such a vast empire, and your begging bowl is so small. Are you worried that I cannot fill it completely with something?" And just to show the beggar, he told the prime minister, "Fill his bowl with diamonds, rubies, emeralds – the most precious stones – so that he will remember for his whole life that he has met an emperor."

There was no problem because the king's palace was full of diamonds and all kinds of precious stones. But immediately there was a problem: the prime minister filled the begging bowl, but the moment anything went into the bowl, it disappeared. The question of filling it completely seemed to be impossible.

But the king was also adamant, an egoist, a conqueror of many lands. He said, "Even if my whole empire is needed, I have given my word and it has to be fulfilled."

Slowly, slowly, all the precious stones disappeared. Then gold, then silver, but they went on disappearing. By the evening, the king himself was a beggar, and the bowl was as empty as it had been in the morning.

The beggar said, "I am amazed. Such a great emperor and you cannot fill a poor beggar's bowl?"

People had been watching the whole day, the rumor spread all over the country. The whole capital had gathered. People from far-away places had rushed to see. The king fell at the feet of the beggar and asked, "I have failed to fulfill my promise; forgive me. But I will think that you have forgiven me only if you tell me the secret of your begging bowl, where the whole empire has disappeared to. All my wealth – where has it gone? Is it a magic bowl? Are you a magician?"

The poor beggar laughed. He said, "No, I am not a magician. By accident, because I didn't have any money even to purchase a begging bowl, I found this skull of some dead man. I polished it, cut it into the shape of a begging bowl. The secret is, man's skull is so small, but even the greatest empire is not going to fill it. It will go on asking for more. I am not a magician, the magic is in the human head. And because of this bowl, I have been hungry for days. Everything disappears and the desire remains the same."

When a man reaches the highest rung of the ladder his whole life is gone, and what does he find there? Nothing – but it needs courage to say it to others who are behind him, struggling to reach the top.

Gautam Buddha renounced his kingdom, not without reason. Mahavira renounced his kingdom, not without reason. The twenty-four *tirthankaras,* the great masters of the Jainas, all renounced kingdoms. They cannot all be mad. But they have seen the reality: their fathers were successful, but successful only in the eyes of others. Others could not see inside them. Inside, they were still beggars, bigger beggars than when they started this journey of ambition. There comes a point when you start feeling that your whole educational system, that your well-intentioned parents, have all been fast asleep.

And there is no way of going back; there is no way of having your youth again. There is no way to let the flowers of love grow in you – you have become dry and hard and dead, because the competition is tough and to be successful you have to be tough. That toughness destroys all your beautiful values – love, joy, ecstasy. You never think of meditation. Money is your only meditation.

The first question comes from a rich man:

Then said a rich man, Speak to us of Giving.

He's asking: "I have struggled and destroyed myself in getting more and more, and now I see that my life began from the very beginning on the wrong track. Please: *Speak to us of Giving.*

"I don't want to get anything more. This whole stupid idea of getting and getting, more and more, has been suicidal. Perhaps by giving I may start feeling a little more alive again. Perhaps a breeze of love may enter into my dark soul, perhaps a ray of light. Getting and getting I have tried – teach me about giving; perhaps that is the right way."

The people in the East who renounce the whole world have inherited a wisdom of centuries: if you want a dance in your heart and peace in your soul, if you want to become more conscious and awake, give it all. It was not *against* the world, as so-called religious teachers of all religions go on teaching people. They do not understand the basic psychology of it. They have seen the great masters renouncing everything, all their possessions, and they have logically concluded that perhaps there is a secret in renouncing. So for centuries they have been teaching against riches, against life, against the world. You can see the ultimate result in the East: it has become poorer and poorer, because if you are going to renounce, then what is the point of first collecting? The East has become a beggar.

But I say unto you: unless you have, how can you renounce?

So Mahavira was immensely blissful, Gautam Buddha was in constant ecstasy – but don't think that a beggar who has nothing to renounce outwardly... He may look like a religious person, but deep down those desires for more – for pleasure, for being special – will go on lurking in the darkness. Gautam Buddha and the people of his type were not wrong. But seeing their joy, their peace, their serenity, an absolutely wrong conclusion has been derived by the scholars, the priests. They go on teaching anti-life values.

This is a simple arithmetic: you can renounce only if you have it. If you don't have... Both persons apparently look alike: one has renounced, one does not have it. Both are in the same situation but not in the same psychology, not in the same spiritual space. Hence, I have been misunderstood all over the world because I have been teaching people: first *have.* And then, if you are intelligent, you are bound to renounce it.

Religion is not for the poor. The poor can pretend to be religious, but inside all those desires for more go on growing. He talks about renouncing, but he knows nothing of renunciation. Renunciation is a second step.

Rejoicing is the first step. Religion happens only to those who have come to the point where they can see that their desires are absurd, they lead nowhere. It has to be your own experience. In that very experience, the psychology of possessiveness disappears; then there is beauty.

Twenty-five centuries have passed and the East has not been able to produce another Buddha. Why? – a tremendously misunderstood logic. The rich man – and *only* a rich man – can ask, "Teach us of giving." A poor man can only ask, "Teach us of getting." In other words, as long as you are asking for more and more, you are poor.

The day the awakening happens to you that this insane idea of getting more and more is not leading you anywhere and your life is slipping out of your hands, then only the question has an authenticity:

Teach us of giving.
And he answered:
You give but little when you give of your possessions.

The words of Kahlil Gibran should be written in pure gold. If you are thinking of giving your possessions, there is not going to be a revolution in your life. Think of giving up your very desire for *possessiveness*. Possessions are not a problem: you can live in a palace, the palace is not going to disturb you. The palace is not even aware of you. The problem is, "It is my palace!" That possessiveness has to be given up; whether you give up the palace or not is irrelevant.

You give but little when you give of your possessions.
It is when you give of yourself that you truly give.

Ambition is the way of the ego. It makes you more and more yourself...

It happened: The first prime minister of India, Pandit Jawaharlal Nehru, had gone to the West for a Commonwealth meeting. His number two in the cabinet was Maulana Abul Kalam Azad. He was given the number two position not because of any special quality, but because he had political power in his hands. The Mohammedans had divided into two: the majority was following Muhammadali Jinnah and asking for a separate land, Pakistan. Maulana Azad remained with the Nationalist Congress, and because of his religious scholarship – a *maulana* is the highest degree as far as Mohammedans are concerned – and because of him, a great number of Mohammedans were not following Muhammadali Jinnah.

Maulana Azad was a great orator, but he knew only Urdu, Arabic. And it is a strange craziness of human beings: the thing that you cannot understand, you think must be of a very high order. All the priests of the world have tried that. The rabbi will speak in Hebrew and the Jews are impressed, although they do not understand anything of it. Translated, it is rubbish. I always have the feeling that the word *rubbish* must have come from *rabbi*, I cannot find any other source. The Hindu pundit will speak in Sanskrit. Neither you know what it means nor perhaps does he know what he is repeating, because translated, it looks so stupid.

All religious teachers have been against their scriptures being translated because once they are translated into the languages which people understand, the power of the priest is gone. If you listen to a Hindu priest reciting from the Vedas, you will be impressed, but look into the translations and you will feel as if you have awakened from a sleep. Perhaps two percent of the sentences in all the four Vedas are significant. Ninety-eight percent are simply crap. And the same is the situation with Buddhism, Jainism and other religions.

Maulana was highly respected, and because of him, India is still the largest Mohammedan country in the world, even after the partition of Pakistan. No other country has as great a number of Mohammedans as India has. Certainly, his power over Mohammedans was great. But he himself was as stupid as every priest needs to be.

He was put second, and he was very annoyed; he wanted to be the prime minister of India. It was so difficult to convince him – "It will look very awkward that the country is being divided in two parts because Hindus and Mohammedans don't want to live together, and then both countries have a Mohammedan prime minister? And Hindus will not tolerate it either. You have taken a large part of the country in the name of religion; now leave Hindustan for those who are in the majority – the Hindus."

He became – reluctantly – ready to be number two because he

knew that in Pakistan he would not even be anywhere. At least here he was number two. But the desire to be the prime minister of the country was such that when Jawaharlal went away, he immediately ordered Jawaharlal's chauffeur: "Now, as long as Jawaharlal is outside the country, I am the prime minister. I am number two in the cabinet: acting prime minister." So the prime minister's car with the prime minister's bodyguards, with the prime minister's flag on the car, other cars ahead, a few other cars behind... He managed the whole prime minister's show in one day.

Other cabinet ministers suggested to him, "There is no such thing as acting prime minister because the prime minister is not the formal head of the government. If the president goes out, then the vice-president becomes acting president for the time being, but the prime minister remains prime minister wherever he is. In no country's constitution is there a provision for an acting prime minister. So it is stupid, don't do it."

But he was not ready to listen. Jawaharlal was informed in London. Immediately, he phoned to Maulana to say, "Don't do such a stupidity, the whole world will laugh. Such a thing does not happen. If you are acting prime minister, then what am I doing here in the prime minister's conference? And the president, who is the nominal head of the country, is there. Just go back to your own bungalow and behave intelligently."

But it is very difficult to behave intelligently if your unconscious mind is filled with desires, with ambitions.

A Gautam Buddha is empty of any ambitions. He has seen the show. But because twenty-four *tirthankaras* of the Jainas, Gautam Buddha, the Hindu reincarnations of God – Rama, Krishna – were all coming from royal families, the richest in the country, it proved a calamity to the whole land. People became poverty-worshippers. If the East is poor, this misunderstanding is the reason. And for centuries, they were conditioned with this stupid logic.

So I say that to be really religious you should live totally and intensely the life of the world, so that you can see one day that it is just a dream. When it is your *own* understanding that it is just a dream – futile, meaningless – the very desire to possess will disappear. You will not ask about giving, because in giving there is still the ego and ignorance present. Who are you to give?

Almustafa is pointing to a very significant fact: you give little if
*...you give of your possessions. It is when you give of yourself that
you truly give.* The moment you are non-possessive, the ego disappears. You have given yourself.

*For what are your possessions but things you keep and guard for
fear you may need them tomorrow?*

All possessiveness – "this is mine, that is mine" – is rooted in
your fear: "Because what about tomorrow?" If you don't cling to
possessions, tomorrow you may be in difficulty.

*And tomorrow, what shall tomorrow bring to the over-prudent dog
burying bones in the trackless sand as he follows the pilgrims to the
holy city?*

The same is the situation of all those who cling to their possessions. A dog, following the pilgrims, hides bones in the sand
without being aware that tomorrow he will not be able to find them
because the pilgrims, the caravan will have moved and he's moving
with the caravan.

Today is enough unto itself. And tomorrow will take care of
itself.

This is trust – not believing in this god, in that god, in this holy
book, in that holy book... The real religious person does not worship, he trusts in existence. Worship is a poor, plastic substitute. He
trusts in existence: he knows, "If existence has taken care of me
today, tomorrow will also be the same. It will come as today, and if
existence needs me, it will take care of me." This is real giving.

*And what is fear of need but need itself?
Is not dread of thirst when your well is full, the thirst that is
unquenchable?
There are those who give little of the much which they have – and
they give it for recognition and their hidden desire...*

All the religions have exploited your hidden desires.

I was participating in a religious conference in Prayag. I heard a
shankaracharya speaking to thousands of people, saying, "If you

give one rupee in donation, in the other world you will get one thousand rupees." A good bargain! Good business! But all Hindu scriptures are full of such promises – "Give a little here and you will get much as a reward in heaven."

This is not trust. This is not getting rid of your mad desire for possessions. Here, you give one rupee, people will see: "This man is a very religious man, he gave one rupee to a beggar." But they don't know his hidden desire. He is giving it as a guarantee so that he can get one thousand rupees after death. He is depositing in God's bank. But the interest rate seems to be absolutely absurd!

People give just a little to make sure that in the other world they will get much. And in this world they will get recognition, respectability; people will think of them as religious people.

One of the successors of Mahatma Gandhi, Vinoba Bhave, went around the country asking people to donate land, just one-sixth of their land to the poor. And he was given millions of acres of land in donation for the poor. Only later on it was discovered that almost all of that land was useless, infertile. But those people got recognition, got seats in the assemblies and the parliament. Not only did they give the rotten land which had no use, they simply *said* it; actually, they never gave it. It had not been transferred to the poor. And what was the poor man going to do with that land? It had no value at all. But this is the way man's ego has invented to get recognition, respectability, honor.

...they give it for recognition and their hidden desire makes their gifts unwholesome.

Kahlil Gibran is truly a religious man with a sincerity, authenticity which is rare. He is saying, "These gifts are not religious. They are unwholesome."

And there are those who have little and give it all.
These are the believers in life and the bounty of life, and their coffer is never empty.

These are the people who trust. If God, or existence, or whatever name you give it, can give you life, its bounty, its abundance will be always available to those who trust.

When I left and resigned from the university, naturally my father was very much concerned. He came rushing from the village which was one hundred and twenty miles away from the university and asked me, "Have you thought of tomorrow? Have you thought of sickness? Have you thought of old age?"

I said, "I never thought of my birth, I never thought of my youth. The same source of life that has taken care, will take care. And if I am not needed, then there is no need to care for me; then I should be removed and a place should be made available for someone who is needed. Don't be worried."

But it was very difficult. He could not convince me, but he did whatever he could. I told him, "Remember, I will not take a single rupee in inheritance from you. You have given me enough – your love, the freedom that you have given me is rare." But a father is a father. He immediately went home and transferred much property into my name, without informing me, because he knew that I was not going to accept it. I came to know about it only when he died. Taxes had to be paid on the property, and for the first time I received a letter saying "You are not paying taxes."

I said, "Have I to pay taxes on my body? Even my clothes don't belong to me. Nothing belongs to me; I don't possess anything, they have come to me from my sannyasins. And I never accept them forever; I accept them only to use – they can take them back any time, they are theirs. I don't use the watch twenty-four hours a day – only for the lecture time, because I don't have any sense of time. I may go on speaking..." And once in a while, when I forget to look at the watch, I do go on speaking. My people have asked, "Should we give you some indication?" I have told them, "Never do such a thing, because I don't like any interference."

I told my father, "I trust existence." And I have proved that existence has taken care of me better than I could have managed myself.

There are those who give with joy, and that joy is their reward.

All the religions have been lying to you – and the police commissioner says to me that I should not criticize any religion! They have lied to you. They say that if you give here, you will be rewarded in heaven. Neither do they have any evidence of heaven nor do they have any evidence from millions of people who have gone before – just a single letter, a postcard, saying, "Yes, what these priests are saying is right."

All the money that you give goes to the priests. But the desire to be rewarded blinds you to a simple truth: in the very giving, you feel so joyful, what more reward is needed?

This is one of the principles I insist on most: that each act comes with either its reward or with its punishment. There is no need of any God who is twenty-four hours noting things in his books about millions of people of this earth. And scientists say there are at least fifty thousand planets where life exists!

Have mercy on poor God, don't burden him unnecessarily. Life has an autonomous mechanism of its own. Your very act is either a reward or a punishment. And that can give you the criterion, too: if it is a reward, it is right; if it is a punishment, it is wrong. If it is a reward, it is virtue; if it is a punishment, it is sin. There is no need to go to anybody to ask. Each act, twenty-four hours a day, is teaching you.

There are those who give with joy, and that joy is their reward.
And there are those who give with pain, and that pain is their
baptism.

This is so beautiful of Kahlil Gibran, that even pain becomes a religious transformation. Even if you give not with joy but with pain, that pain will purify you. That pain is a fire, it will burn all that is wrong in you. You will come out of it more sincere, more human, more religious. This is the meaning of baptism – not the baptism of the Christian priests.

And I am going to criticize it: dropping a little water on small babies' heads is not baptism, it is simply foolishness.

I have heard a story...

A great bishop lived opposite a great rabbi, and naturally there was continuous competition. Even in religious people the same thing continues.

One day the rabbi came out in the morning and saw that in front of the bishop's porch there was sitting a beautiful Chevrolet, the latest model. And the bishop came out and sprinkled water on it. The rabbi could not resist his temptation – what was this idiot doing?

He went and asked, "Dear sir, what are you doing?"

The bishop said, "Baptism – now the car is Christian."

The rabbi was very much offended by the new Chevrolet, but a rabbi is a Jew, intelligent as far as money is concerned. He managed that night to collect enough money to purchase a beautiful Lincoln Continental, a much higher-class car than the Chevrolet. The Chevrolet in America is the poor man's car. The Lincoln Continental is their best car – the rich man's car.

The bishop saw it from his house. He said, "My God, this rabbi is something!"

He went to the rabbi's house and asked, "Whose car is this?"

The rabbi said, "Whose? I have purchased it. It is the latest model Lincoln Continental."

And the bishop said, "What are you doing?" With garden scissors he was cutting the exhaust pipe.

He said, "I am doing the circumcision – now it is a Jew."

And these idiots are not only in stories, they are realities spread all over the world.

A real baptism is the fire through which you pass, the pain through which you pass. Don't escape it. Still trust in existence: if it gives you pain there must be some reason for it, something in your heart has to be burned so that you can become pure.

And there are those who give and know not pain in giving, nor do they seek joy – these are the purest, the most religious – *nor give with mindfulness of virtue.* They don't give because giving is taught by every religion as virtue.

They give as in yonder valley the myrtle breathes its fragrance into space.

They give just like flowers give their fragrance to the winds, to take it wherever the wind is going. They never come to know to whom they have given. They are not concerned. They simply give out of their love for no reward, for no virtue. These are the highest givers. They are not even aware of giving.

Through the hands of such as these God speaks, and from behind their eyes He smiles...

They have become one with existence. Their hands are God's hands and their eyes are God's eyes.

Through the hands of such as these God speaks, and from behind their eyes He smiles upon the earth.

These are the highest peaks of consciousness, beauty, love. Everybody has the potential to become the hands of God, the eyes of God. And unless you become that, you have missed the very point of your life.

It is well to give when asked, but it is better to give unasked, through understanding...

Why humiliate a person and force him to ask? That is ugly. When you see that some need exists and you are able to fulfill it through your own understanding, fulfill it.

When I was a student in the university, I used to receive two hundred rupees per month from someone, I knew not who. I had tried every way to find out who the person was. On the first day of each month, the money order was there but there was no name, no address. Only when the person died... And he was no one other than the founder of the university in which I was a student.

I went to his home. His wife said, "I am worried. Not because my husband has died; everybody has to die. My concern is, from where am I going to get two hundred rupees to send you?"

I said, "My God, your husband has been sending it? I never asked, and there was no need because I am getting a scholarship from the university, free lodging, free boarding – everything free."

The wife said, "I also asked him many times: 'Why do you go on sending two hundred rupees to him?' And he said, 'He needs it. He loves books but he has no money for books. His need for books is greater than his need for food.'"

But he was a rare man. In his whole life, whatever he earned he donated to create the university in his town.

India has almost one thousand universities. I have seen many. His university is small; it is a small place. But his university is the most beautiful – on a hilltop surrounded by great trees, and below it such a big lake full of lotus flowers. The lake is so big that you cannot see the other shore. And I came to know that he had given everything to the university. Nobody was asking, nobody was even expecting that in that small place there would be a great university.

He was a world-known legal expert. He had offices in London, in New Delhi, in Peking; he was continuously on the move.

I had asked him, "Why have you chosen this place?"

He said, "I have gone all over the world and I have never seen such a beautiful small hill, with big trees, with such a beautiful lake, with so many lotuses."

The whole lake was covered with flowers and lotus leaves. In the early morning, on all the lotus petals... Dewdrops gathered in the night; in the morning you could see that lake was the richest in the world because each dewdrop shone like a diamond.

He had taken me around the place and he said, "It is not a question of my town, it is a question of the beauty of this place."

But I had never imagined that he would be sending me two hundred rupees per month, unsigned. So I could not even send him a thank you note.

It is well to give when asked, it is better to give unasked, through understanding;
And to the open-handed the search for one who shall receive is joy greater than giving.

What can we give? Everything is mundane.

Almustafa is right when he says that the true giver is not concerned to attain some joy by giving. His joy is in searching for someone to whom he can give who is receptive, who is open, who will not feel offended.

And is there aught you would withhold?
All you have shall some day be given;
Therefore give you now...

Death will take everything away. Hence, never be worried about giving. Life has given to you, life will take it away. Why miss the chance of the joy of giving? Why miss the chance of becoming the hands of God, and the eyes of God?

...that the season of giving may be yours and not your inheritors'.

People collect for their inheritors. This is wrong for two reasons: one, you miss the chance of giving; secondly, whoever is going to inherit your money will miss the chance of earning it himself. You have destroyed two persons – yourself and your children.

6

WORK
making your love for existence visible

And what is it to work with love?

It is to weave the cloth with threads drawn from your heart, even as if your beloved were to wear that cloth.

It is to build a house with affection, even as if your beloved were to dwell in that house.

It is to sow seeds with tenderness and reap the harvest with joy, even as if your beloved were to eat the fruit.

It is to charge all things you fashion with a breath of your own spirit,

And to know that all the blessed dead are standing about you and watching.

Often I have heard you say, as if speaking in sleep, "He who works in marble and finds the shape of his own soul in the stone, is nobler than he who ploughs the soil.

"And he who seizes the rainbow to lay it on a cloth in the likeness of man, is more than he who makes the sandals for our feet."

But I say, not in sleep, but in the over-wakefulness of noontide, that the wind speaks not more sweetly to the giant oaks than to the least of all the blades of grass;

And he alone is great who turns the voice of the wind into a song

made sweeter by his own loving.
Work is love made visible.
And if you cannot work with love but only with distaste, it is better
that you should leave your work and sit at the gate of the temple
and take alms of those who work with joy.
For if you bake bread with indifference, you bake a bitter bread that
feeds but half man's hunger.
And if you grudge the crushing of the grapes, your grudge distils a
poison in the wine.
And if you sing though as angels, and love not the singing, you
muffle man's ears to the voices of the day and the voices of the
night.

Almustafa is saying immensely beautiful things but the most important thing is missing. That is the misery of a poet: he comes to know as deeply as possible but he never reaches the very center. Only a mystic is able to reach to the very center, so although all these statements are beautiful, keep in mind that something is missing. And I am going to make you aware of what is missing.

I am not a poet. I can understand the beauty of poetry because I am a mystic; I am rooted in my own center, in my own being. I would love you to understand Almustafa's statements – perhaps they will help you reach to the center, of which he himself is not aware.

And what I am saying about Almustafa, I am really saying about Kahlil Gibran. I have not spoken on him. For many years, again and again, I thought to give new blood and new life to his statements, but whenever I saw that there was something missing, I wondered whether I would be doing justice to you if I simply commented on Kahlil Gibran without telling you that he is not an enlightened man. Very close – but even closeness is a distance. Unless you become one, the distance remains. But finally I decided that it is better to make Kahlil Gibran and his spokesman, Almustafa, complete and whole.

And what is it to work with love?
It is to weave the cloth with threads drawn from your heart, even as
if your beloved were to wear that cloth.

It is a very loving attitude toward work, but still it is not work that arises out of love because the beloved is separate. And the one who is beloved today may not be tomorrow. The love that humanity knows can easily turn into hate. The ordinary love is a double-edged sword. When you are in love with someone – it may be God, but it does not mean that your love cannot turn into hate any moment.

Once a man came to me and said, "I am a great believer in God."

I said, "I have seen you before. You were always complaining against God, what has happened?"

He said, "I was complaining because I didn't have a child. And I was continuously praying for ten years and God had not responded to my prayers. I stopped praying, I stopped going to the temple. I felt cheated, deceived. It became clear to me that there is no God.

"But I was impatient. Just yesterday a child was born. I wanted to inform you first – because you know of my ten years of misery – that I am greatly happy. God *is*. Though he may delay his decisions for his own reasons which we know not, the prayer is always heard; if not today, then tomorrow."

I said, "You are still impatient. The child can also die. What will happen to your love and your trust and your belief in God? With the death of the child your God would also die. He is born with the child and he would be gone with the child. You would hate him more than ever. Before, he was just not listening to your prayers, but now he has taken away your long, long desired child."

He said, "Don't say such a thing!"

I said, "I have to say it to make you aware that your love for God is seasonal. Just like the seasonal flowers – for weeks they are there dancing in the wind, and within weeks they are gone. Your love has not arisen from the center of your being. It is not an experience, it is just a bribe."

And, by the way, I would like you to know that it is very difficult to destroy the ugly existence of bribery from this land, because this land has been bribing even God for thousands of years.

People go to the temples and they say, "If our desires are fulfilled we will offer you sweets, fruit. We will believe in you. The fulfillment of our desires is the only evidence that you exist."

That's why I say Kahlil Gibran is not yet a mystic. First, let us hear what Almustafa is saying:

It is to weave the cloth with threads drawn from our heart...

The heart is better than the head, but you are not the heart, you are still deeper: you are the being, eternal being. The moment your head dies, your heart will also stop beating. Your head and your heart both belong to the body and to the world.

Only you, in total purity of consciousness, belong to the eternal flow of life. Only you belong to existence. And if you are basing your belief on some desires which are fulfilled, it is better than to believe because certain arguments have convinced your head – but it is not yet the real thing.

You should love, not because of any reason; you should love because you are so overflowing with love. It should not be addressed to the beloved. And you all know your love goes on, up and down. The enemy can become the friend, the friend can become an enemy. You are not free, it depends on the object.

Your love is freedom only when it does not depend on any object but simply flows from your being for no cause at all. That's why it cannot be changed. It is going to be eternal. Whether God exists or not makes no difference, whether there is any beloved or not makes no difference. You will still be loving.

It is not a question of loving someone, it is a question of being love yourself. That does not come from the heart, it comes from a very deep source, the ultimate depth of your being, and it showers over all: the deserving, the undeserving, the worthy, the unworthy. It makes no discriminations.

But that kind of love arises not because you have a beloved; that kind of love arises because you have reached to your very innermost center. It comes out of meditation; that is the missing point. Otherwise, it is a beautiful poetry and what he is saying is significant:

It is to build a house with affection, even as if your beloved were to dwell in that house.

This is the poverty of the poet. Once in a while he makes the effort to reach to the stars but he goes on falling back to the earth again and again. His poetry is mixed – sometimes it reaches to the open sky on the wing and sometimes it creeps on the earth. And unless you are a meditator you will not be able to make the distinction because his words are always beautiful. Just see: he is saying, *It is to build a house with affection...* but from where are you going to get affection?

And he says: *even as if...* Remember those two words *as if.* It is all imagination: *even as if your beloved were to dwell in that house.* As if? – you are trying to create a hallucination around yourself.

When you see a beautiful sunset you don't say, "Look, it seems as if the sunset is very beautiful." Your "as if" is your doubt, your "as if" is simply your inference.

Just think: you love a woman or a man and you say, "It seems as if I love you." Do you think this is going to convince the woman? If she's really a woman and not a bogus lady, she is going to hit you hard! As if!

But the difference is clear: the mystic speaks with an authority. The poet, at the most, can speak always rooted in ifs and buts.

There is a great book by a very famous philosopher; its name is *As If.* The man is sincere. He does not say, "God exists." He says, "*As if...* I think God exists."

Beware of ugly words like *as if.* Either you love or you don't love, there is no middle ground.

It is to sow seeds with tenderness and reap the harvest with joy,
even as if your beloved were to eat the fruit.

The words are beautiful but the content, the substance, is on shaky ground. That *as if* means you are making a castle in the sand, believing that no wind is going to destroy it. But the winds don't follow your orders.

The religious man never uses the words *as if.* It is the philosopher, the poet, it is the blind person who thinks, "As if there is light." He has not seen it, he has heard about it. Everybody is talking about it; perhaps they are right. But it is not his own direct experience, and unless the experience is direct and yours, it is not liberating. It is going to create a bondage. It will make you a dreamer, but dreams need sleep and unconsciousness.

It is to charge all things you fashion with a breath of your own spirit,
And to know that all the blessed dead are standing about you and watching.

This seems to have some truth, at least in this city of the dead. But I will not call them *the blessed dead*. There is only one blessing and that is life. It is pure mannerism, etiquette, that you call the dead "the blessed." Then what are you doing here? Why don't you die and become blessed? Living, you are cursed – and a cursed man, once dead, becomes "the blessed."

Just the other day I told you that this is a temple of a living god. If you come here, come with your total being and participate with the people in their joy, in their song. But still I have seen on the chairs – or have you removed the chairs? – a lady... I will not call her a woman because *woman* is a respectable word; a lady is just bribed by the male chauvinists to function almost like the dead. I have seen one woman not participating in your song and in your joy. I don't see many dead people here; just one poor woman keeping herself apart, afraid to be joyous, afraid to merge and meet you in spirit.

I will have another look when I leave, whether the miracle has happened or not. In the past it used to – Jesus called Lazarus and after four days of living as dead, he immediately came out alive. There are still two hours for the dead lady to become a living woman.

And do you know, the word *lady* is ugly. It means a good lay. And the lady is supposed to lie down while making love, almost dead – not moving, not showing her joy, not screaming. This is a very cunning strategy of man because he knows the woman can have multiple orgasms. One man can have only one orgasm; his love is finished within two, three minutes. By that time, the lady has not even become warm enough, what to say about hot dogs?

For thousands of years, the woman has been exploited in such cunning ways. She has been told, "This is being graceful, to lie as dead and suffer the whole agony." That's why all women, when you are making love to them, close their eyes. They don't want to see what is happening because they are not participants. Otherwise it is the most beautiful dance of meeting, of merging, of two lovers in oneness.

I cannot support the statement: *And to know that all the blessed dead are standing about you and watching.*

But in a Christian conditioning – Kahlil Gibran is a converted Christian, his forefathers changed their religion from Mohammedanism to Christianity. All the religions born outside of India believe that you have only one life – and then sit on trees, blessed, dead, or stand, as you wish, and watch for eternity until the last day comes, the Day of Judgment.

Jesus was asked again and again, "When is the Day of Judgment coming?" Because his apostles were greedy, they wanted to enter paradise as soon as possible. And Jesus lied to them, or perhaps he himself was living in an illusion.

He said, "Very soon. In your very life you will see the gates of paradise flung open. I will be standing with my father, God, indicating who has followed me – he will be allowed in. And those who have not followed me will fall into the eternal darkness of hell."

This small statement made Bertrand Russell, who was born a Christian, very irritated and annoyed. He dropped out of Christianity and wrote a book, *Why I Am Not A Christian*. Of all the reasons that he has given, this is the most important: that the whole religion is just without any sense of justice.

In one life, how many sins can you commit? If you go on committing sins every moment – without eating, without drinking, without sleeping, for seventy years non-stop – even then you cannot commit enough sins in seventy years to deserve eternal hellfire. Eternal! There should be some justice.

Bertrand Russell himself said, "I have committed many things which can be condemned by Christians as sin and I have dreamed many things which can be also condemned as sin. My actions and my dreams both could be joined together, and the hardest judge could not send me to jail for more than four or five years."

Eternal condemnation to hellfire with no exit, no way of coming out, is sheer stupidity, nonsense, unreasonable. But a man like Kahlil Gibran is still burdened with the idea.

[A man in the audience, a visitor, rises to leave the hall.]

Look at this man... Where are you going? And if you were going to leave this place, why have you come? These are the dead people! Look at his face, and the woman I indicated – they should not be allowed in. This is a congregation, this is not a film show!

But all the religions that have been born in India are more rational in this sense. They do not believe in one life but in reincarnation. You go on being reborn again and again. The whole eternity is given to your life, without any beginning and without any end.

So I have been watching in the morning – I don't see any dead soul watching from the trees. Just a few dead souls enter out of curiosity, or perhaps they are in plainclothes, just police dogs. But I will not tolerate anybody who is here out of curiosity, who is here as an observer, who is here as a detective, who is here as an informer. And you all have to be aware. Whenever you see somebody not participating, this is the last time he has entered this temple of godliness.

Often have I heard you say, as if speaking in sleep...

But that *as if* goes on. He's not certain what he is saying. He is simply assuming – *as if speaking in sleep:*

"He who works in marble and finds the shape of his own soul in the stone, is nobler than he who ploughs the soil."

Painters, poets, sculptors, dancers are being awarded with Nobel Prizes. Have you heard that a gardener who creates life, beautifies life, has received a Nobel Prize? A farmer, who plows the field and brings nourishment to you all – has he ever been rewarded? No, he lives and dies as if he has never been here.

This is an ugly demarcation. Every creative soul, it does not matter what he creates, should be respected and honored, so that creativity is honored. But even politicians get Nobel Prizes – who are nothing but clever criminals. All the bloodshed that has happened in the world has happened because of these politicians and they are still preparing more and more nuclear weapons to commit a global suicide.

In a real, honest human society, creativity will be honored, respected, because the creative soul is participating in the work of existence.

"And he who seizes the rainbow to lay it on a cloth in the likeness of man, is more than he who makes the sandals for our feet."

Our sense of aesthetics is not very rich.

I am reminded of Abraham Lincoln. He was the son of a shoemaker and he became the president of America. Naturally, all the aristocrats were tremendously disturbed, annoyed, irritated. And it is not a coincidence that soon Abraham Lincoln was assassinated. They could not tolerate the idea that the country had a shoemaker's son as the president.

On the first day, when he was going to give his inaugural address to the Senate, just as he was going to stand up, an ugly aristocrat stood up and he said, "Mr. Lincoln, although by some accident you have become the president of the country, don't forget that you used to come with your father to my house to prepare shoes for our family. And there are many senators who are wearing the shoes made by your father, so never forget your origins."

He was thinking he was going to humiliate him. But you cannot humiliate a man like Abraham Lincoln. Only small people, suffering from inferiority, can be humiliated. The greatest of human beings are beyond humiliation.

Abraham Lincoln said something which should be remembered by everyone. He said, "I am very grateful to you for reminding me of my father just before I give my first address to the Senate. My father was so beautiful, and such a creative artist – there was no other man who could make such beautiful shoes. I know perfectly well, whatever I do, I will never be such a great president as he was a great creator. I cannot surpass him.

"But by the way, I want to remind all you aristocrats that if the shoes made by my father are pinching you, I have also learned the art with him. I am not a great shoemaker, but at least I can correct your shoes. Just inform me, I will come to your house."

There was great silence in the Senate, and the senators understood that it was impossible to humiliate this man.

But he had shown a tremendous respect for creativity. It does not matter whether you paint, sculpt, or make shoes; whether you are a gardener, a farmer, a fisherman, a carpenter – it does not matter. What matters is, are you putting your very soul into what you are creating? Then your creative products have something of the quality of divine.

Except creativity, there is nothing divine.

But I say, not in sleep, but in the over-wakefulness of noontide, that the wind speaks not more sweetly to the giant oaks than to the least of all the blades of grass.

Existence treats everyone equally. The sun does not rise only for the rich people; neither is the full-moon night dedicated to the presidents and prime ministers of the world. When the wind blows and brings fragrance, it does not bother whether you are a famous man or just a nobody.

Existence is pure communism, it treats everybody equally. The saint and the sinner are not demarcated. The water will not say to the sinner, "You cannot quench your thirst because you are a sinner. I am here for the saints." Just learn something from existence, because this is the only holy scripture. I don't know any other scripture which is holy – but nature is innocent, pure, sacred.

If we had listened to nature, man would have been part of this tremendous equality: respect for all, reverence for life. But man has forgotten the ways of nature, he has become absolutely unnatural. His misery is a by-product of his being unnatural.

And he alone is great who turns the voice of the wind into a song made sweeter by his own loving.

But you will not find the names of those people in your history books because they were not murderers on a great scale – like Alexander the Great, who killed for no reason at all; just an idiotic desire to conquer the whole world. These conquerors cannot be creators. They are the most destructive people in the world. The whole world's pressure is on Ronald Reagan to stop creating more nuclear weapons. But he seems to be absolutely insane. He is not listening to anybody. And these American politicians have been condemning the Soviet Union continuously. But the Soviet Union, seeing the stubborn attitude of Ronald Reagan, has stopped creating more nuclear weapons ten months ago. This needs courage.

Ronald Reagan and his company are a company of cowards. Now what is the point? – when the Soviet Union was also creating nuclear weapons, there was some point: "Don't be left behind." The Soviets tried their best to convince them: "We are ready to reduce our nuclear weapons; you start reducing yours in the same proportion." Seeing that there is no possibility from a religious bigot and a political fanatic like Ronald Reagan, they themselves have stopped – alone. This has raised their prestige all over the world.

Ronald Reagan is already a defeated soul. You have shown your cowardliness, and all your propaganda against the Soviet Union seems to be nothing but lies.

You will be surprised to know that I have been expelled from America for no reason, and the Soviet Union has invited me to their international book fair and said that if I cannot come, I can send somebody with all my literature: "We want the Soviet Union to know all the best literature of the world."

In America, nearabout one million dollars' worth of my books were being sold every year. But suddenly no bookseller, no chain stores – who were continually saying, "your supply is not enough for our demand" – are ready to put my books in their showcases. Who is a fascist country today? America has turned into a far more fascist country than the Soviet Union or Germany has ever been.

And Ronald Reagan is a very religious person, he is a fundamentalist Christian. What kind of religiousness is this? He is deceiving the beautiful American people and he is trying to destroy the whole world. The world has never before seen a worse criminal in power. Adolf Hitler has been left miles behind. But these names make history: Genghis Khan, Tamerlane, Nadir Shah. They have only destroyed.

I am reminded of Nadir Shah – he had invaded India, and each night he wanted beautiful women and wine. The whole day he was killing people, and at night there was a celebration.

One night, his soldiers brought a prostitute who was very beautiful. She danced, and Nadir Shah was very happy. In the middle of the night, he said, "I am feeling tired, and tomorrow morning we are going to invade another country. So stop the dancing."

But the frail, young and beautiful woman said, "In the dark night, passing through a forest, I will have to go to my village. At least allow me to stay overnight. In the morning, when there is light, I can go."

He said, "Don't be worried. You are a guest of no ordinary person; you are a guest of Nadir Shah. I will make your path full of light right now!" And he ordered his soldiers to set alight all the villages along the way, set all the trees alight along the way, so the prostitute could go in full light. Twenty villages, with living beings who were asleep, were set alight and the whole forest was set alight to create a morning in the middle of the dark night – just for the prostitute to walk, because she was no ordinary person's guest.

These are names which make history. You will never, in your history books, come across those who are humble, silent, peaceful.

But Kahlil Gibran is right: *And he alone is great who turns the voice of the wind into a song made sweeter by his own loving.*

Except a loving heart, there is no greatness anywhere. And you all have a loving heart. You just have to be told that it needs to be opened, made available to existence – to life, to people, to trees, to oceans, to everything that surrounds you.

Work is love made visible.

Whenever you create, you are making your love for existence visible. But your religious saints are telling you to renounce the world.

In India, there are thousands and thousands of monks – of Hindus, of Jainas, of Mohammedans – but they are all uncreative. They don't even paint or write poetry. No, work is condemned, and these people who are the condemners of life and its creativity are worshipped.

I have been asking people, "Where are you going?" And in India, to go to a saint is called *seva* – service. They are going to serve the saint. The saint cannot work, cannot create, is the most useless person – an unnecessary burden on a poor country – and he needs service.

I used to know a very beautiful man, Magga Baba. He was so tired of these people continuously serving him, because there is a limit to everything. They wouldn't let him sleep! If ten persons were massaging him, he was such a simple, innocent soul that he would not say anything. "Let them do..."

But one night he disappeared. He used to disappear – not on his own accord. He was perhaps the only person who was continuously being stolen – because one village had served him enough, some other village, finding the chance, would steal him. And he would not say anything. If they said to him, "Sit in the rickshaw," he would sit there.

Many times he was found in different villages and brought back. But finally he got so tired...

I was a university student in those days, and once in a while I used to go to him – just to sit by that silent man, because he never used to speak to anybody. But I was blessed that, if there was no one else, he would whisper something into my ear. And the last thing he whispered in my ear was: "Tears are coming into my eyes because I will not be able to see you again."

I said, "What happened? Any indication of being stolen?"

He said, "No, I have got so tired of all these people who are serving me. I cannot sleep, so I am just going to disappear in the mountains. And I will not be coming back because humanity is not the place to live silently."

He was an enlightened being. But no history book will ever mention him. History seems to be obsessed with the murderers, with the powerful, with people who have created all kinds of nuisance in the world and have not been a help or a blessing but a curse.

If a new humanity arises, the first thing is to make bonfires of all the history books. Get rid of Alexander the Great, Napoleon Bonaparte, Ivan the Terrible, Adolf Hitler, Joseph Stalin, Benito Mussolini, Ronald Reagan. Don't let your children's minds be poisoned by these people!

History should take note of the creators, of people who are nobodies, but because of their nobodiness they have turned into flutes – hollow bamboos. The wind blows and the flute turns the wind into a song. These are the people who love existence because they beautify it.

But all religions are against life. They say, "Renounce life," and life includes work, life includes love, life includes everything. "Renounce life, because your renunciation of life is going to be an entry into paradise after your death." But it is always *after* death.

All the religious people and the politicians are angry with me for the simple reason that I am telling people that life is *herenow* – not after death; don't wait. And life is in love, life is in being creative, life is in understanding your innermost being. Because only then can you become a constantly overflowing source of beauty, love, and joy.

Who cares about life after death? Life is *before* death, and if you can live totally there is no death for you. This is the experience of all those who have entered into silence. They have witnessed the greatest miracle: that their innermost core, their consciousness, is eternal. Life can take away the clothes, the bodies, but life cannot destroy *you*. But only the creator – and a creator out of love – transcends death.

Work is love made visible.
And if you cannot work with love but only with distaste, it is better
that you should leave your work and sit at the gate of the temple
and take alms of those who work with joy.

If you cannot be a creator, if you cannot love work, if you cannot love life, then the only possibility for you is just to be a beggar. The lover is an emperor, the creator is an emperor – without invading the whole world. He has invaded the whole universe out of sheer, loving creativity. But if you cannot do that, then at least just sit before the temple as a beggar.

Why is he particularly suggesting the temple? Because if the temple is a living temple – and I mean by a living temple one where the master is still alive – there will be seekers coming, lovers, creators, and you will be constantly seeing that they are human beings as you are. Perhaps you may start feeling ashamed of being a beggar. Perhaps one day you may wake up and enter the temple, not as a beggar but as a seeker of truth, as a seeker of love, as a learner of how to create.

For if you bake bread with indifference, you bake a bitter bread that
feeds but half man's hunger.
And if you grudge the crushing of the grapes, your grudge distils a
poison in the wine.
And if you sing though as angels, and love not the singing, you
muffle man's ears to the voices of the day and the voices of the
night.

The song is continuous. The birds are singing, the flowers are singing. Whether you can hear it or not is a different matter. You think the flowers are not singing? You should think that you are deaf! Because I have heard them singing, dancing. Even in the dark night, the silence is a song. If you cannot do anything, at least allow existence to enter into your being. It will transform you.

I call the science of transformation, meditation.

Just sitting here, listening to the birds, is being filled with the eternal creativity.

I had been in this garden for seven years before I went to America. My people had planted small plants and now it has become really a jungle, so beautiful that you need not do anything – just sit silently under the shade of a tree and feel what trees are whispering to each other. There is constant communion between the earth and the sky.

And if you have heard that whispering, your heart will start dancing with joy. That whispering will become your song of life. That whispering will make you understand the Song of Solomon.

It is a strange fact that in the Old Testament, which is the holy book of the Jews... They don't allow the New Testament in their holy book; the New Testament concerns Jesus and his teachings. In the Old Testament, there is only one thing which has any spiritual significance and that is the *Song of Solomon*. But Jews are very much afraid that people should know about that song. It is not discussed in their synagogues because it is a song of life – not of renunciation but of rejoicing. It is a song of love. That is the only part of the Old Testament which is *really* religious. The Old Testament, without the *Song of Solomon*, has no worth, no value at all.

But the rabbis and the synagogues and the scholars are all concerned with the Old Testament and somehow feel ashamed that the *Song of Solomon* is there – what to do with it? And it is the only beauty in the whole Old Testament, the very essence of spirituality.

7

FREEDOM
the innermost substance of freedom

And an orator said, Speak to us of Freedom.
And he answered:
At the city gate and by your fireside I have seen you prostrate
yourself and worship your own freedom,
Even as slaves humble themselves before a tyrant and praise him
though he slays them.
Ay, in the grove of the temple and in the shadow of the citadel I
have seen the freest among you wear their freedom as a yoke and a
handcuff.
And my heart bled within me; for you can only be free when even
the desire of seeking freedom becomes a harness to you, and when
you cease to speak of freedom as a goal and a fulfillment.
You shall be free indeed when your days are not without a care nor
your nights without a want and a grief,
But rather when these things girdle your life and yet you rise above
them naked and unbound.

And how shall you rise beyond your days and nights unless you
break the chains which you at the dawn of your understanding
have fastened around your noon hour?

In truth that which you call freedom is the strongest of these
chains, though its links glitter in the sun and dazzle your eyes.

The true freedom has nothing to do with the outside world. The true freedom is not political, is not economic; it is spiritual. Political freedom can be taken away at any moment; economic freedom can disappear just like a dewdrop in the early morning sun. They are not in your hands. And that which is not in your hands cannot be called true freedom.

True freedom is always spiritual. It has something to do with your innermost being, which cannot be chained, which cannot be handcuffed, which cannot be put into a jail. Yes, your body can suffer all these things, but your soul is intrinsically free. You don't have to ask for it, and you don't have to struggle for it. It is already there, this very moment. If you turn inward, all chains, all prisons, all kinds of slaveries disappear – and there are many. Freedom is only one; slaveries are many – just as truth is one, lies can be thousands.

And an orator said, Speak to us of Freedom.

The orator is only articulate with words. He talks about freedom, about love, about beauty, about good, but he only talks; his oratory is nothing but a training of the mind. The orator has no concern with realities. His world consists only of words – which are impotent, without any content – and his art is to manage those impotent and contentless words in such a way that you are caught in the words.

It is very relevant that an orator asked Almustafa, *Speak to us of freedom.*

What exactly is the innermost substance of freedom? – that you are free from the past, that you are free from the future. You do not have memories binding you to the past, dragging you always backward – that is against existence: nothing goes backward. And your freedom is also from imagination, desire, longing – they drag you toward the future.

Neither the past exists nor the future exists. All that you have in your hands is the present.

The man who lives in the present, unburdened of past and future, knows the taste of freedom. He has no chains – chains of memories, chains of desires. These are the real chains which bind your soul and never allow you to live the moment that is yours. As far as I am concerned, I don't see that without a meditative mind one can ever be in freedom.

In India, what you have known in the West as paradise is known as *moksha. Moksha* means freedom. Paradise does not mean freedom, paradise comes from a Persian root, *phirdaus,* which means "a walled garden." But don't forget that it is a *walled* garden: it may be a garden, but it is a prison.

The biblical story says that God became annoyed with Adam and Eve and threw them out of the Garden of Eden. Into what? Where? If you ask me, it was a curse hiding the greatest freedom, the greatest blessing. They were out of the prison, and that was the beginning of humanity. Now the whole sky and the whole earth was theirs, and it was up to them what they make of it. It is unfortunate that they have not been able to create a free world. Each nation has again become a walled prison – not even a walled garden.

In a small school, the religious teacher was talking to the children about the biblical beginnings of the world. A small boy raised his hand to ask a question. The teacher asked, "What is your question?"

He said, "My question is: the Bible says, 'God drove out Adam and Eve.' What model of car did he use?"

It must have been a Ford – the first model, called the Model T Ford. And I think that poor God is still driving the Model T Ford without any mechanic, because neither his son Jesus Christ is a mechanic, nor is the Holy Ghost, nor is he himself.

Christianity thinks that God punished man. My understanding and insight says: God may have thought he was punishing them, but the reality is that God is still imprisoned in a walled garden. And it was a blessing in disguise that he made man free. His intention was not good, but the result was the whole evolution of man. And if evolution is not going as fast as it should go, again the priests of God, of all religions, are preventing it.

When Galileo found that it is not the sun that goes around the earth, that it is an appearance and not a reality... The reality is just the opposite: the earth goes around the sun. When he wrote a treatise explaining his reasons, evidence, proofs, arguments, he was very old – seventy or seventy-five – and sick, bedridden, almost dying. But

Christian love is such that the pope's people dragged him from his bed to the court of the pope.

The pope said, "You have committed the gravest crime, because the Bible says, and everybody knows, that the sun goes around the earth. Either you have to change your opinion, or the penalty will be death."

Galileo, even in his old age, sick and dying, must have been an immensely beautiful man, a man with a sense of humor. He said, "Your Honor, there is no problem. I can write what you are saying. There is just one thing I want to make clear to you – that my writing is going to be read neither by the sun nor by the earth. They will continue in their old way, as they have always done. The earth will continue to go around the sun. You can burn my book or I can change the paragraph."

The pope said, "Change the paragraph."

He changed the paragraph and wrote, "According to the Bible and according to the pope and according to the ordinary humanity, it appears that the sun goes around the earth." And in the footnote he wrote, "The truth is just the opposite. I cannot help it – I cannot convince the earth to follow the Bible, and I cannot convince the sun to follow the Bible. They are not Christian." The footnote was discovered only after his death; otherwise he would have been crucified by the Christians – who go on making so much fuss about the crucifixion of Jesus.

I was talking to one of the most important Christian missionaries, Stanley Jones, and asked, "What do you think about it? Why was the pope insistent? If science had discovered it, the Bible should have been corrected."

Stanley Jones said to me, "It may have great implications. If one statement in the Bible is wrong, then what is the guarantee that other statements are not wrong?"

And the Bible is a holy book, coming directly from God. Nothing can be changed in it, nothing can be edited out, nothing can be added to it. And in the last three hundred years man has found so many things which are against the Bible.

In fact, as you grow in consciousness, you are bound to find that what was written two thousand years ago, or five thousand years ago, has to be continually improved. New editions have to be produced. But what religions lack is courage – courage to be on the side of truth. And it is not only Christians, the same is the case with the Hindus, the

Mohammedans, the Jews, the Buddhists, the Jainas. There is no difference in their mentality.

A man of freedom is free of the past. And the man of freedom is also free of the future, because you don't know what is going to happen the next moment. How can you go on desiring?...

An old man was dying. He was a Jew; and his four sons, who used to live in different houses, were of course immensely rich people. Hearing that their father was dying, they rushed to him.

Their father was dying, taking his last breath on the bed and, just sitting by the side of the bed, the sons started discussing how to take his body to the graveyard. Their concern was not their father – a few minutes more and he would be gone, forever; there was no possibility of their meeting or recognizing each other again. But that was not their concern. They were concerned about: "When he dies, how are we going to take his body?"

The youngest boy suggested, "He always wanted to have a Rolls Royce. And he has enough money, we have enough money; there is no need for him to suffer and repress an innocent desire. So at least we should bring a Rolls Royce to carry his body to the graveyard. In his life he missed, but at least in death he will have a Rolls Royce."

The second boy said, "You are too young and you don't understand matters concerning money. It is a sheer wastage, he is dead. Whether you take him in a Rolls Royce or in a truck does not matter to him. He will not be able to know, so why waste money?" And it was not much money either, just to hire a Rolls Royce taxi. It was not a question of purchasing it. He said, "My suggestion is that a cheap truck will do as efficiently as any Rolls Royce – for the dead it makes no difference."

The third boy said, "You are also still immature. Why bother about a truck when the municipal corporation truck takes, free of charge, any beggar who dies? Just put him out on the road! In the morning the municipal truck, with all kinds of rubbish, will take him for free. Give him a free ride! And what does it matter to a dead man whether it is a municipal truck or a hired truck or a Rolls Royce?"

At that very moment the old man opened his eyes and asked, "Where are my shoes?" They were puzzled, "What are you going to do with shoes? Why waste a pair of shoes? Anyway you are going to die."

He said, "I'm still alive and perhaps have a few more breaths.

Just bring the shoes; I will walk to the graveyard. That is the cheapest and the sanest way. You are all extravagant, spendthrift."

People may have money, and the money becomes their fetter. People may have prestige, and the prestige becomes their fetter. It seems the whole past of humanity has been improving on how to make better chains, but even if a chain is made of gold, it is still a chain. Freedom on the outside is just the politician's continuous deceiving of the whole humanity.

Freedom is your individual affair. It is totally subjective.

If you have thrown out all the rubbish of the past and all desires and ambitions for the future, this very moment you are free – just like a bird on the wing, the whole sky is yours. Perhaps even the sky is not the limit.

Why is the orator, not a slave, asking him? It would have been far more relevant had a slave asked: *Speak to us of Freedom.* The orator is asking about freedom so that he can start speaking on freedom with more efficiency and with more articulateness.

He is not interested in being free. His interest is to become a great orator *about* freedom – because everybody is in chains of different kinds, and enslaved by religions, by politicians, by parents, by society. The orator is simply asking to decorate his speeches. It is not an authentic question. But the answer is far more authentic. Almustafa answered:

At the city gate and by your fireside I have seen you prostrate
yourself and worship your own freedom.

What do you do when you go to a Hindu temple, or a Mohammedan mosque, or a Christian church, or a synagogue? – you are worshipping things which you yourself have created. And that shows man's utter stupidity: first you carve a statue of God and then you prostrate yourself before it. This is your religion. Why don't you start touching your own feet? There is no difference.

Mohammedans have been in difficulty because Mohammed, fourteen centuries ago, found that the people of Arabia were worshipping three hundred and sixty-five statues. Kaaba was their temple, and for every day one statue was worshipped. And even Mohammed, uneducated, could see the foolishness of it – you make the statues, and then you worship them – so he destroyed all those three hundred and sixty-five statues.

I am not in favor of his destruction. Instead... The same thing started again. He himself started it, because he found man is so much in love with his own misery that he cannot understand the idea of freedom – because to be free is to be free of misery.

The same Kaaba, where three hundred and sixty-five statues used to exist, also had a big square stone. It was not an ordinary stone, it was an asteroid. Every night you see stars falling – but stars don't *fall,* and it is good and compassionate of them that they don't fall because they are so big that if they fell on the earth the whole earth would disappear as if it had never existed. What you see, and call falling stars, are nothing but small stones.

When the moon became separated from the earth, at first the earth was not so solid. It is not solid even today. If you go deep inside... Deep inside it is burning lava. Once in a while it erupts into a volcano, but the upper crust has become solid. In the beginning it was not solid, and when the liquid earth was first moving on its own center...

It takes twenty-four hours for it to move on its own center. And then it is also moving around the sun – it takes three hundred and sixty-five days. In this double movement parts of the liquid crust were falling out here and there. Where you find, today, the great oceans, those are the places where big lumps of earth fell out. Joined together, they became your moon.

This moon continues to move around the earth, but no religious scripture of the world has any idea of it. Sometimes, because there are almost three thousand stones falling every twenty-four hours onto the earth... In the day you cannot see them because the sun is so bright, but in the night you can see them. It is a stone moving toward the earth, pulled by gravitation, with such speed that the friction makes it burn up; hence you see the light and you think it is a star.

But sometimes big stones also fall, and Kaaba is one of the biggest stones that has fallen. Because it had fallen from above, the people who worshipped the three hundred and sixty-five statues thought that it was a gift from God, and they placed it in the middle of the temple. The temple was vast – naturally, to accommodate three hundred and sixty-five guests. It was a five star hotel! And it was just a coincidence that the stone of Kaaba fell there. Mohammed destroyed all the statues, but he could not destroy men's memories, he could not destroy men's imaginations. Not finding the statues, they started worshipping that great stone.

It seems that man is afraid to be free. He wants some father in the sky, at least for complaints and prayers. He needs a father in the sky as God to take care of him. Without God in the sky he feels like a lost child. It is a father fixation, psychologically.

Almustafa is saying, "I have seen you worshipping and prostrating yourself; and in a certain way you worship yourself – in a roundabout way." The simplest way would have been to just put a mirror up, stand before the mirror, and with folded hands, repeat any kind of prayer – Hebrew, Sanskrit, Arabic, Greek, Latin. Don't use the language that you know, because when you know the language your prayer looks very ordinary. When you don't know the language, it is mystifying.

Even as slaves humble themselves before a tyrant and praise him though he slays them.

Your worship is just like slaves praising the tyrant who has reduced them from humanity into slavery. And he can kill them any moment, because a slave is property, not a person.

Ay, in the grove of the temple and in the shadow of the citadel I have seen the freest among you wear their freedom as a yoke and a handcuff.

Thousands of years of many kinds of slavery have made you so afraid to be free – which is your birthright and which is your ultimate blissfulness. Your so-called temples and synagogues and mosques and churches are not symbols of freedom, they are symbols of your slavery, of your dead tyrants. But even intelligent people go on doing the same thing.

For example, I would like to tell you... Mahatma Gandhi has been praised all over the world. Perhaps I am the only person who can see his retardedness: he was preaching nonviolence his whole life and at the same time he was worshipping the *Shrimad Bhagavadgita*, the Hindu bible, which is the only book in the world which teaches violence. And I cannot conceive that he could not see the contradiction.

Krishna, in the *Bhagavadgita*, says continually to Arjuna, "It is God's will that you should go to war and destroy your enemies." But because it was a family quarrel – they were cousin-brothers fighting with each other, Arjuna and Duryodhana – it was a very strange kind of fight. On each side they had their relatives. It was one family – even the grandfather had to choose which side to be on; even their master, who had taught both of them the art of archery, had to choose.

Bhishma is known as one of the great men in India, because he remained celibate his whole life. And Dronacharya, the master archer, had loved Arjuna, because he had the capacity to become a master archer in his own right. But still, both of them, the wise Bhishma and the great archer Dronacharya, chose to be against Arjuna and his brothers, because they were only five brothers, and the other party consisted of one hundred brothers. Dronacharya and Bhishma's choice to be on the other side shows not wisdom but only a business mind. Seeing that the one hundred brothers had more strength - and it is always good to be with the strong.

Almost the whole country was divided into two parts. There were friends on that side, there were friends on this side. Even Krishna was in a difficulty – he was the spiritual guide of the whole family. So he found a way and gave a choice to both Arjuna and Duryodhana: "One can have me and the other can have my armies. You can choose." Naturally Duryodhana chose his big army, and Arjuna chose Krishna himself to be his charioteer.

The day of fight had come. Both parties, millions of people, had gathered on the war field, facing each other. A strange kind of fight – they were all related in some way or other to each other. Seeing the whole thing, Arjuna said, "I don't feel this victory is worth anything. Killing my own people, because on the other side are also my own people – my grandfather, my teacher, my friends, my relatives – and on my side also are my friends. Both will be killed.

"And even if I become victorious, upon millions of corpses, sitting on a golden throne, I will not be happy. These are the people I have loved, these are the people I have lived for. And just for the kingdom and a golden throne...? I am feeling very sad and, seeing the truth with my own eyes, I want to renounce the world and become a sannyasin and go to the Himalayas. Let my cousin-brothers rule – at least nobody will be harmed.

"How can I kill my own master, who is on the other side? How can I kill my own grandfather, who is on the other side?" And Krishna went on and on to convince him, "A warrior's religion is to fight. You are becoming weak, you are becoming soft. A warrior need not have any heart."

But no argument could convince Arjuna. Finally, as the last resort, Krishna said, "It is God's will that you should participate in the war." If I were in the place of Arjuna, I would not have wasted that much time – because why should God speak to Krishna and not to Arjuna – "If it is his will, he should speak to me directly. I'm feeling that it is absolutely ridiculous and I'm going to take sannyas and move to the mountains to meditate."

But we have always accepted mediators: God speaks through the pope, God speaks through Jesus Christ, God speaks through Krishna. He has a certain kind of postal system; he never speaks directly.

The whole book of the *Bhagavadgita* is full of arguments for violence – even God is for violence. My puzzle has been that Mahatma Gandhi, teaching nonviolence, continually carried the *Bhagavadgita* with him. He worshipped the *Bhagavadgita*; every morning a part of it was recited in the ashram of Mahatma Gandhi. And he never became aware of the fact that it is the only book in the world which teaches so openly in favor of violence, and even drags God into it. Man's blindness seems to be unlimited.

So if you have been in chains, handcuffed, for thousands of years, you must have started believing, "These are ornaments, this is the will of God." Your parents cannot be your enemies. If they take you to the church or to the temple, they take you there because they love you. But the reality is, they take you there because they were taken by their parents. It is a robot-like process, mechanical. And slowly, slowly the slavery has penetrated into your blood, into your bones, into your very marrow.

So if somebody speaks against Krishna, immediately you are ready to fight with him: he has spoken against your God, who is nothing but a slavery. If somebody speaks against Jesus, immediately you are furious: he has spoken against your God – but he was speaking only against your chains.

This is the reason I have been condemned by all the countries of the world, all the religions of the world – because I'm speaking against their slavery. It is polished, decorated, and they have always lived in it: their parents and their parents' parents, a long line of slaves. How can they drop their inheritance? You get in inheritance nothing but slavery. And even if you don't take it seriously, still it is serious.

I have heard...

Three rabbis were talking about their synagogues. The first rabbi said, "My synagogue is the most advanced because in my synagogue, while I am delivering the sermon, people are allowed to smoke, gossip, talk. I have given them total freedom."

The other two rabbis laughed. The second one said, "This you call advancement? Come to my synagogue. I have given them freedom to drink alcohol, and when they become drunk they shout, they scream, they fight, but I continue giving my discourse. This is freedom."

In a synagogue women and men cannot sit together; there is a curtain between them. And the second rabbi also said, "The curtain has been removed. Now women and men sit together. I don't even interfere, whether it is your wife you are sitting with or not. Even boyfriends and girlfriends are allowed to do all kinds of loving things – kissing, hugging – and my discourse continues. We have entered into the era of freedom."

The third rabbi said, "You are both idiots. You should come sometime to my synagogue. I have placed a board in front of the synagogue, saying that on every Jewish holiday the synagogue will remain closed. This is freedom. Why waste people's time? At least on a holiday let them have all kinds of entertainment available to them."

But these are not freedoms. They are all still Jews. Unless you drop your Jewishness, your Hinduism, your Jainism, your Mohammedanism, unless you are completely clean of the past, unless you are no longer dominated by the dead and no longer enchanted by the unpredictable future, you are not free. Freedom is here and now – neither the yesterday nor the tomorrow, but this very moment.

A man of understanding unburdens himself. And all the chains that have been heavy on his heart – although he had become accustomed to that heaviness – disappear.

I am saying it to you with absolute authority, because it is my experience. The moment your chains disappear you start growing wings for the sky. Then the whole sky, full of stars, is yours.

And my heart bled within me; for you can only be free when even the desire of seeking freedom becomes a harness to you...

A very profound statement: The very desire for freedom can also become a fetter. All desires fetter you; freedom is not an exception, for the simple reason that all desires live in the future. A man who is free does not even know anything about slavery or freedom, he enjoys his freedom. It is his very quality of being.

And my heart bled within me; for you can only be free when even the desire of seeking freedom becomes a harness to you, and when you cease to speak of freedom as a goal and a fulfillment.

All goals are bound to be in the future, and all desires for fulfillment in the future are nothing but a cover-up of your misery in the present. Your tomorrows go on giving you promises – it is only one day, it will pass; tomorrow I will be free. But tomorrow never comes, has never come. You will never be free. Tomorrow is only a consolation. Instead of bringing freedom to you, it is going to bring death to you. And all the days that you lived, you lived as a slave, because you never bothered about the present.

I say unto you that the present is the only reality there is. The future is your imagination, and the past is your memory. They don't exist. What exists is the present moment.

To be fully alert in the present, to gather your consciousness from past and future and concentrate in the present, is to know the taste of freedom.

You shall be free indeed when your days are not without a care nor your nights without a want and a grief...

It seems man has fallen into such a trap. He is not even as free as the birds of the sky, or the wild animals of the forest. There are so many fetters around him, and he has accepted them. In fact, what is your care right now? What is your anxiety right now? What is your anguish right now?

In this silence, you are absolutely free.

When your days are free of care, your nights are bound to be without grief, because the same day is reflected in your nights. If the whole day you are disturbed and worried, and hankering and desiring and feeling frustrated, your nights will be nightmares. But if you are living each moment in its totality, with intensity, with your wholeness, your nights will be calm and quiet, relaxed and peaceful. Not even a dream can disturb you, because dreams come from unfulfilled life, from repressed life.

The Western psychology has missed the point completely – particularly psychoanalysis; it goes on analyzing your dreams without bothering about the source. The source is in your waking hours, but you are so fettered, so imprisoned in your religion, in your morality, in your etiquette, in your manners, that you cannot live. All these unlived moments will return to you when you are asleep, because anything unlived slips into your unconscious. If you are living fully...

Freud would have been very surprised if he had come to the East, and gone to see the aboriginals who live deep in the forests. I have visited them, and the most surprising thing is that they don't have any dreams. They know the real depth and relaxation of life. Naturally, in the morning they are more alive, younger, more fresh, to face the day and to live it again totally. The condition of the civilized man is just the opposite. He not only dreams in the night. Anytime, sit in your chair, relax and close your eyes, and some dream starts floating by.

You are not living. You only desire to live. You are hoping to live someday, hoping that this night is not going to be forever, that sometime there must be dawn. But for the slave there is no dawn. He has to live in darkness, without even becoming aware that there is such a thing as light.

Don't take your so-called life for granted. This is not life at all. You have to go through a revolution; and that revolution has nothing to do with any politics, with any economics. It has something to do with your spirituality and an awareness – when your innermost core is full of light, your outer light also starts reflecting it.

You shall be free indeed when your days are not without a care nor your nights without a want and a grief,
But rather when these things girdle your life and yet you rise above them naked and unbound.

Because they are old, and old companions to you, they will

again and again try to make you unfree. But you should be aware always to transcend them. You should watch them coming, and say good-bye to them forever. That is, to me, the essential meaning of sannyas. Then suddenly you become part of these beautiful trees, with beautiful roses, with great stars – they are all free.

Except in man, there exists no slavery in the world. And to get out of it is not difficult. It is not a question of your slavery clinging to you. The reality is you are clinging to your slavery.

It happened one time: I was standing by the side of a great river, in full flood, and it looked like a blanket was going down the river. One man, a fisherman, immediately jumped to catch hold of the blanket, and the moment he got hold of the blanket, he started shouting, "Save me, help me!"

I could not understand it. I said, "I don't understand it. If the blanket is too heavy, drop it.

He said, "It is not a blanket, it is a living wolf, and I saw only his back and thought it was a blanket."

I said, "Then leave me alone."

But the situation of your slavery is not that of the fisherman; it is not that your slavery is clinging to you. The fisherman was in a difficulty, because now the wolf was clinging to him.

Your chains are *your* responsibility. You have accepted them; they are there. In full awareness, say to them, "Good-bye, you have been long with us. It is enough, we depart." A simple awareness is needed to bring freedom to you, but there are some vested interests in clinging to your slavery.

I was a teacher in a university, and for almost twenty days I was out of the town, moving around the country. That much leave is not possible; although, within ten days of every month, I was completing the course with the students. I asked them, "Have you any complaint?"

They said, "We are grateful to see the fact that for a small course, two years are wasted. No more than six months is needed." But the vice-chancellor became disturbed, because again and again he found that I was not in the university.

I had my own device: there were beautiful trees, but strangely, all the trees had died. There was only one tree which was still green and with shade, so I used to park my car under that tree. It had become known that nobody should park his car there. Once or twice people had tried, and I had called my students to remove the car – wherever it goes, let it go, but this place is reserved! So whenever I was going out of the town I used to send my car with my chauffeur, and the vice-chancellor, seeing my car under the tree from his window, was satisfied that I was there.

One day he was taking a round of the whole university, and he found my class was empty. He asked the students, "He is supposed to be here, and his car is parked exactly under the tree. And I have been always suspicious: I have been reading his discourses – sometimes in Kolkata, sometimes in Amritsar, sometimes in Madras – and I have always been puzzled; his car is there."

I used to drive my car, and I had told my chauffeur, "Lock the car and enjoy yourself for one or two hours in the garden, and then take the car back home."

The chauffeur asked, "Well, what is the point?"

I said, "Don't be worried about it; it is not your problem."

So one day, when I came back from Madras, the vice-chancellor called me and asked, "It seems you are a master of yourself. You never ask for leave, you never even inform me."

I said, "Just give me a piece of paper," and I resigned.

He said, "What are you doing?"

I said, "That is my answer. Are my students suffering in any way by my absence? Have they said to you that their courses are not complete? It is sheer nonsense to waste two years of their lives. My job is to teach them their full course. It does not matter in how many days I do it."

In the evening he came to my house, and he said, "Don't leave us."

I said, "What has happened, has happened, and I cannot enter your university for the simple reason... Just see, I have burned all my certificates, because I don't want bridges with the past. I will never need those certificates. Now I am an uneducated man."

He said, "I will not say anything to anybody."

I said, "That is not the point. I really wanted to resign, but I was simply waiting – it should come from you, not from me."

Almustafa is saying:

But rather when these things girdle your life and yet you rise above them naked and unbound.

My father was worried, my friends were worried. My students came, saying, "Please take your resignation back."

I said, "That is impossible. I don't have any qualifications to be your teacher anymore."

My father was saying to me, "Even if you have resigned, what is the point of burning all your certificates and qualifications?"

I said, "What is the point of keeping them? Keeping them means somewhere deep down, the desire is still there: perhaps you may need them, cling to them. I am now completely free of all that education, which has not given anything to me. And I don't want to carry those wounds – they are not certificates – always with me."

After two years the vice-chancellor asked me, "At least once in a while you can come to address the whole university." So I went. He took me into his room, to the window from where he used to see my car. He said, "A strange phenomenon – only that tree was green. Now it too has died."

I said, "Life is mysterious. Perhaps the tree had fallen in love with me, perhaps the tree was living just for me, because for nine years continually my car was waiting under the tree, and I had become very friendly with the tree. It was not only a question of parking the car under it, I always thanked the tree. Once in a while, when my chauffeur was with me, sitting at the back, he would say, "You are really crazy – thanking the tree?"

I said, "The tree is so loving. Out of all the trees in the line, it is a very beautiful tree – *gulmarg*, with red flowers. When spring comes you can only rarely see the leaves; there are so many flowers that the whole tree becomes red." The other trees of the same kind had all died, but she remained with me, alive for nine years. Still somebody else parks his car there, but perhaps he has not even bothered to thank the tree, has not shown his gratitude to the tree.

The moment you are free of past and future, just sit by the side of a tree, whisper something to the tree, and soon you will know that it responds. Of course, its response is not going to be in words; perhaps it showers its flowers on you; perhaps it dances in the wind. And if you are sitting very close, your back touching the tree, you will start feeling a certain new sensation that you have never felt before. The tree is vibrating with love for you.

This whole existence is full of love, full of freedom – except miserable man; and nobody is responsible for it except you. And it is not a question of gradually dropping. Many people have come to me and said, "We understand you; gradually we will drop." But slavery is never dropped gradually: either you have understood and you are free, or you have not understood and are just pretending to understand.

Freedom does not come in fragments, neither does slavery go in fragments. When you bring a light into a dark room... Have you not seen it? – does the darkness go in fragments: a little part, then another part, making a queue, going out of the room? Or does the light come in fragments: a little light, then more, then more? No, the moment you bring the light in, there is no darkness. The very understanding of what freedom is – and you are free. It is not a question of time, or gradualness.

And how shall you rise beyond your days and nights unless you break the chains which you at the dawn of your understanding have fastened around your noon hour?

There is no other way. You started all those chains in your very childhood, perhaps in the name of obedience, in the name of your love for your parents, in the name of trust in your priests, in the name of respect for your teachers – good names. Always remember to remove the label and see what the content is inside, and you will be surprised: slavery is being sold to every child in beautiful names. It will be difficult for you to drop it, unless you see that it was not the slavery that you were attached to, it was the label that was given to it.

It was a constant fight with my father. He was a loving man, very understanding, but still he would say, "You have to do it." And my response would always be, "You cannot say to me, 'You have to do it,' you can only suggest, 'If you like, you can do it; if you don't like, you are free.' It has to be basically my decision, not yours. I am obedient toward the truth, toward freedom. I can sacrifice everything for truth, for freedom, for love, but not for any slavery. Your 'should' stinks of slavery."

Soon he understood that I don't belong to the obedient or the disobedient. I am not saying, "I will not do it," I am simply saying, "Withdraw your 'should.' Give me space to decide whether I want to say yes or no, and don't feel offended if I say no.

"It is my life, I have to live it, and I have every right to live in my own way. You are much more experienced; you can suggest, you can advise, but I am not going to take orders from anyone. Whatsoever the cost, whatsoever the consequence, I am not going to take orders from anyone."

And slowly, slowly he dropped his "should." He started saying, "There is this problem. If you feel right, you can help me; if you don't feel like helping, it is your decision."

I said, "This is what real love should be."

In truth that which you call freedom is the strongest of these chains, though its links glitter in the sun and dazzle your eyes.

What do you call freedom? – mostly the political, the economic, the outside freedom which is not in your hands, which has been given to you. It can be taken away. Only that which has grown within you cannot be taken away from you; hence, Almustafa says:

In truth that which you call freedom is the strongest of chains, though its links glitter in the sun and dazzle your eyes.

It happened in Uruguay: the president had been reading my books, listening to my tapes, and he was very happy to welcome me to become a permanent resident in Uruguay. All the forms were ready. He had given me a one-year, permanent residency card, so that all the bureaucratic procedure was fulfilled, and nobody could say that I had been favored. And he said, "Then I would like to give you three years' permanent residency, which will turn automatically into your citizenship."

Uruguay is a small country, but very beautiful. I asked him, "Why are you interested in me? – because all the governments are passing orders that I should not enter their countries. Not only that, my airplane cannot land at their airports.

He said, "They don't understand you."

The day the president was going to sign the forms, the American ambassador was watching continually, and the American government dogs of the CIA and FBI were following me everywhere. Their plane was either ahead of me or behind me. When they saw that he was going to sign for a permanent residency, which would turn automatically into citizenship, they immediately informed Ronald Reagan.

Ronald Reagan phoned the president of Uruguay, and said, "My message is not big, it is small: either force Osho to be deported within thirty-six hours from your country, or I will cancel all the loans for the future that we have agreed on" – which amounted to billions of dollars – "and I will demand back all the dollars that we have given to you as loans in the past. If you cannot pay, then their interest rate will be doubled. You are perfectly free to choose."

I have never seen such a soft-hearted person. With tears in his eyes, he said, "Osho, I am utterly helpless. For the first time, your coming to Uruguay has made us aware that we are not free. Our country is economically a slave. Our sovereignty, our freedom is just fake. These are the alternatives given to me.

"I asked Ronald Reagan, 'What is the need to deport Osho? I can simply ask him to leave – because for deportation, when he has a one-year permanent residency, he would have to commit a heinous crime like murder, only then could he be deported.' But Ronald Reagan insisted, 'I have said what I wanted to say – he has to be deported.'"

The president's secretary came running to me and said, "It is better that your jet plane leaves from a small airport, not from the international airport, because the American ambassador is there to see whether you are being deported or not."

It was an absolutely illegal demand, a criminal demand: a man who had not left his room, all the days I was there.

I asked, "On what grounds can you deport me?"

He said, "There is no question of demand, no question of any law. It seems that for you, law does not exist."

The president arranged my flight, just because he was feeling so guilty. He was going to give me citizenship, and now he is deporting me for no reason at all. But those American government dogs, seeing that my jet plane had moved from the international airport... Where could it go? They immediately came to the small airport and forced the president to send all the necessary papers for deportation. I was delayed for two hours. The papers had to come, they had to be filled in to show that I was deported; my passport had to be stamped that I was deported.

My passport is really a historical thing. I have told my people to preserve it. The twenty-first century is coming, and exactly twenty-one countries have deported me, without any reason.

My attorney came running. He said, "This is absolutely illegal, we can fight it in court."

I said, "I will not fight with a man who had tears in his eyes and felt so wounded, so humiliated: '...because we cannot pay the debts, and we cannot afford the rejection of future loans.'"

Political empires have disappeared from the world, not because of your freedom struggles but because imperialists have found an easier way of keeping you enslaved while giving you the superficial idea that you are a flowering, independent, free country.

All these people use very beautiful words – they are "helping." First, the poor countries used to be called, just three years ago, "undeveloped" countries, but that word, *undeveloped*, hurts the ego. Now they are called, "developing countries." Just the word has changed, but "developing countries" hides the wound. They are all economically enslaved.

A man's life is small. Don't waste it in any other kind of freedom. Be decisive about it: you have to be free in your soul, because that is the only freedom there is.

8

REASON AND PASSION
no longer in conflict

And the priestess spoke again and said: Speak to us of Reason and
Passion.
And he answered, saying:
Your soul is oftentimes a battlefield, upon which your reason and
your judgment wage war against your passion and your appetite.
Would that I could be the peacemaker in your soul, that I might
turn the discord and the rivalry of your elements into oneness and
melody.
But how shall I, unless you yourselves be also the peacemakers,
nay, the lovers of all your elements?

Your reason and your passion are the rudder and the sails of your
seafaring soul.
If either your sails or your rudder be broken, you can but toss and
drift, or else be held at a standstill in mid-seas.
For reason, ruling alone, is a force confining; and passion,
unattended, is a flame that burns to its own destruction.
Therefore let your soul exalt your reason to the height of passion,
that it may sing;
And let it direct your passion with reason, that your passion may

*live through its own daily resurrection, and like the phoenix rise
above its own ashes.*

*I would have you consider your judgment and your appetite even as
you would two loved guests in your house.*
*Surely you would not honor one guest above the other; for he who
is more mindful of one loses the love and the faith of both.*
*Among the hills, when you sit in the cool shade of the white
poplars, sharing the peace and serenity of distant fields and
meadows – then let your heart say in silence, "God rests in reason."*
*And when the storm comes, and the mighty wind shakes the forest,
and thunder and lightning proclaim the majesty of the sky, – then
let your heart say in awe, "God moves in passion."*
*And since you are a breath in God's sphere, and a leaf in God's
forest, you too should rest in reason and move in passion.*

Humanity has suffered more because we have lived in divisions, than for any other reason.

Man is one organic whole. This has to be your fundamental understanding: there is no way to cut off any of your parts and yet remain blissful. Yes, all those parts have to be brought into a harmonious whole, just like an orchestra. So many people are playing on different instruments, and if they don't know how all those different instruments should melt and be one, in one music, then there is not going to be music at all only noise, which will not be soothing to your soul but a disturbance.

Man's whole history is the history of divisions. Discard this, discard that, and just cling to one part of your being. You will remain in misery, because bliss is born when all your parts are dancing together in a deep harmony, without any conflict.

Why has man created this schizophrenic state of mind? It is not without reason. It is the device of those who want to dominate you, those who want to exploit you, those who want you to remain enslaved forever. A man who is whole cannot be oppressed, cannot be exploited and cannot be reduced to a slave. And there are people whose only ambition is for power; power seems to be their only cause for living.

Friedrich Nietzsche died in a madhouse. It is an unfortunate thing: while doctors were declaring him mad, priests were declaring him mad, his own friends and family were declaring him mad, he was writing his greatest book – in the madhouse. The name of the book is *The Will to Power.*

Looking at the book and its greatness, anyone can see that all those people who forced him into the madhouse were simply trying to get rid of someone whose every word was an arrow. They were not able to bear the height of his being. They wanted him to be completely forgotten and ignored. Certainly he was not mad; otherwise the greatest book of his life could not have been written in the madhouse. He himself never saw the book published – it was published posthumously.

I have looked into all his works. It seems in *The Will to Power* he has put together everything that was scattered in the many books of his writings. Each statement is so pregnant that it is impossible for a madman to have written it. It is so logical, so profound, that if you are ready to read it without any prejudice, you will be amazed that one of the best books in the world was written by a madman, in a madhouse.

His only fault was that he was not obedient to the society or its out-of-date disciplines, rotten rules. His crime was simply that he was an individual in his own right – and slaves cannot tolerate a man who knows freedom, and lives freedom. His actions and his words are out of freedom, but the slaves feel irritated, annoyed, because they cannot even understand what he is saying. He is shouting from a hilltop to the people who are creeping in the dark valleys of their so-called comfort. They are in the majority, and this man is disturbing them on each point that they have been clinging to as wisdom. He is proving that it is sheer stupidity.

Kahlil Gibran was immensely impressed by Friedrich Nietzsche. Nietzsche opened the heart of humanity in his work, *The Will to Power:* why is there no music, but only misery? The reason is that the priests of all religions, and politicians of all kinds of ideologies, are so desirous of power that they don't want humanity to listen to a man who is talking of unity, inner harmony, being undivided, one and whole.

Yes, there are going to be changes, because things in your being have been put by the society in such a way that you are in a mess: the servant has become the master, the master is being treated as a servant. The heart cannot shout, it only whispers; the mind shouting loudly makes it completely impossible for the heart to give his message to you.

Kahlil Gibran is making these very important statements through the mouth of a fictitious mystic poet and philosopher, Almustafa. I have always wondered why he chose to speak indirectly, and my feeling is absolutely clear about it: he did not want to suffer the same fate Friedrich Nietzsche suffered – and nobody is serious about poetry. Friedrich Nietzsche wrote prose; although his prose is so beautiful that you can call it poetry. But he was speaking directly to humanity.

Almustafa created a fiction. Kahlil Gibran was never declared mad, was never forced to live in a madhouse, for the simple reason that he was only a fiction writer – at the most a composer of poems. He secured himself by hiding behind Almustafa. So I want you to remember, whatever words Almustafa says are the words of Kahlil Gibran.

And the priestess spoke again and said: Speak to us of Reason and Passion.

...of mind and of heart, of logic and of love.

For centuries man has thought of them as opposed to each other. He has been told by the vested interests that if you listen to both, you are going to be mad – they are contradictory; you will have to choose.

Those who choose reason have all the opportunities to be powerful in the world, but are empty inside. Those rare souls who choose passion, love, the heart, are aflame inside with beauty, blissfulness, fragrance, but on the outside they have no power.

The priestess is asking one of the fundamental questions:

Speak to us of Reason and Passion.

What is your approach to these two things? Both exist in man, and they appear – at least superficially – contradictory. A choice has to be made; otherwise man will be riding on two horses, and the ultimate result cannot but be a disaster.

She was not aware that Kahlil Gibran has a far deeper insight than the priests and the priestesses, the politicians and the people who have power – either of money or of prestige.

And he answered, saying:
Your soul is oftentimes a battlefield...

...because you have never gone to the roots of your being.

Reason says one thing, the heart longs for something else, and whatever you choose you will suffer, you will remain miserable, because half of your being will remain starved, hungry. Slowly, slowly, the distance between the two will become so great, as if you have been cut in two parts by an electric saw.

These split people are fighting within themselves; they have become a battlefield. This is a strategy, a very cunning strategy. If a man is put in a situation where he is fighting with himself, he has neither energy nor time to revolt against slavery, against oppression, against exploitation. His inner fight has made him so weak that anybody can dominate him. It is a subtle way of psychological castration.

Man has been made impotent with a very clever device. If you are together and one, you have the integrity, individuality and energy to fight against anything that wants to destroy your freedom. And if all humanity has that integrity, dictators will disappear. Politicians have no place in a right human society. In a cultured society, what is the need of laws, of courts? The judges, the police commissioners lose all their power. So as not to lose the power, they have to keep you divided.

Nietzsche spoke directly, and suffered for it. Nietzsche is one of the greatest sacrifices humanity has made – because of power-hungry people. But they are not bothered about Kahlil Gibran. People will read him as a poet, a beautiful entertainment, but nothing more.

Your soul is oftentimes a battlefield, upon which your reason and your judgment wage war against your passion and your appetite.
Would that I could be the peacemaker in your soul, that I might turn the discord and the rivalry of your elements into oneness and melody.
But how shall I, unless you yourselves be also the peacemakers, nay, the lovers of all your elements?

Whatever is given to you by existence cannot be without a hidden purpose. You have reason: reason has eyes, capacity to think, to find out the right part. You have the heart and all its passions, but the heart knows how to sing, how to dance, how to love. The heart cannot create science and technology, neither can reason create love, peace, silence – all the qualities that make you transcend ordinary humanity.

The heart can give you the wings for transcendence and the flight of the alone to the alone. The heart is the door to where godliness can be found. Reason is absolutely incapable. It can create money, it can create thousands of other objective things, but it has no capacity to enter into your inner world.

There is no need for any conflict. Reason functions in the objective world, and the heart functions in the subjective world. And if you are alert, meditative, you can easily manage a balance between the two.

I have called your heart the Zorba, and the flight of your intelligence – which is nothing but refined energy of reason – Gautama the Buddha. Until now, Zorba and Buddha have been fighting. Both are losers, because the Buddha does not allow total freedom for the Zorba; neither does the Zorba allow the Buddha any life of his own.

So there have been Zorbas in the world – all their smiles, all of their joy, is without any depth; it is not even skin deep. And there have been buddhas whose joy is profound, deep – but there is a constant disturbance from the Zorba because the Zorba does not want to starve. There is no difficulty in bringing them closer, to create a friendship between the two and finally a deep oneness.

There is an ancient story... Two beggars, one was crippled and could not walk, and the other was blind but could walk. Of course, they were competitors. Begging is a business where there is continuous competition – you don't know which beggar owns you. When I came to know it, it was a great surprise. Because I was traveling continually, I was coming and going to the railway station so many times, an old beggar had become accustomed – in fact, he had started taking it for granted – that whenever I came back from a journey, or went for a journey, he was entitled to have one rupee.

In the beginning he used to be grateful. When I, for the first time, gave him one rupee, he could not believe it – Indians don't give rupees to beggars. But slowly, slowly, everything becomes taken for granted. Now it was not a question of gratitude, it was a routine. And I could see from his eyes that if I didn't give him a rupee he would be angry – I was depriving him of a rupee.

I never deprived him, but one day I was surprised: the old man was gone, and a young man was sitting in his place and he said, "Don't forget that one rupee."

I said, "How did you come to know about the one rupee?"

He said, "You don't know... I got married to that old beggar's daughter."

Still I could not understand, "If you got married, where is the old man?"

He said, "He has given me the whole area of the railway station as a dowry, and he has given me all the names – your name is the first name. You have been giving him one rupee each time, whether you enter the railway station or you come out."

I said, "This is a revelation, that beggars have their territories." They own it. They can give it as a dowry to their sons-in-law. I said, "This is great! Where is the old man?"

He said, "He has found another place near a hospital, because the beggar who used to sit there has died. And he looks old, but he is a very strong man. Nobody wants to fight with him." Beggars are also in continual conflict to own the clients, customers.

Both the beggars were born enemies, but one day... They lived outside the town, in the forest. In the middle of the night, the forest went on fire. There was nobody to save them. The cripple knew that the fire was coming closer and closer, and all the trees were going to be burned; but he could not walk. And the blind man felt intense heat rising. This was for the first time they spoke to each other in friendly terms: "What is happening? – you have eyes, you can see." And they came to a compromise, forgetting all their fights of the past.

The blind man said to the crippled one, "Sit on my shoulders, so that we become one man. I have enough strength to carry you, and you have eyes to see where to go, where to find a way out of this constantly increasing fire." And they were both saved.

The whole town was awake and they were worried about the beggars, but nobody was courageous enough to enter the forest to find out where they were. They knew that one could not walk. They knew that the other could not see, but they had not thought of the possibility that they could become one. And when they saw them coming out of the forest alive, they could not believe their eyes. What a miracle had happened!

This is an old, very old story. India has one of the most ancient books of parables, *Panch Tantra*; this story comes from *Panch Tantra*. And this is the story of you, about you. The house is on fire, death is coming closer, but you are not yet one solid individual; you are a battle field inside yourself.

Reason can see, but alone, seeing is not of much help. The heart can feel, but alone, feeling is not much of a help. Is it possible that seeing and feeling are no longer competitors, but join in an adventure for the search of the meaning of life?

That is what Kahlil Gibran is saying: "I know the remedy, but, *unless you yourself be also the peacemakers, nay, the lovers of all your elements*, this miracle is not possible."

Hence, I have been proclaiming the new man as Zorba the Buddha – which is a meeting of East and West, which is a meeting of science and religion, which is a meeting of logic and love, which is a meeting of the outer and the inner. Only in these meetings will you find peace; otherwise, you will remain a battlefield. If you are miserable, remember that the misery is arising out of an inner battle that goes on day in, day out.

There have been great Zorbas in the world. "Eat, drink and be merry" is their simple philosophy. "There is no life beyond death. God is nothing but an invention of cunning priests. Don't waste your time on unnecessary things; life is short."

In India we have a whole philosophy, the system of the Charvakas. Perhaps a Charvaka is the most articulate Zorba, and if you try to understand him he is very convincing: "There is no evidence, no eyewitness of any God or of any life after death. There is no evidence or proof that you have an immortal soul. Don't get caught in these words, which have been created just to create a conflict in you so you can become Christians, Hindus, Jainas, Buddhists, Mohammedans."

India has also known great buddhas. They say the world is illusory; all that is true is inner, and all that is untrue is outside. So don't waste your time in desires, in ambitions, they are nothing but the same stuff as dreams are made of. Use the small time that you have in your hands to go as deep inside as possible so that you can find the temple of God – your godliness.

If you listen to the buddhas, they seem to be convincing. If you listen to the Zorbas, they seem to be convincing – and then you are in trouble because you have both within you.

I want you to be a peacemaker, not a battlefield. Let there be a deep friendship between your reason and your passion, so that you can enjoy what is available on the outside – and much is available. It is not illusory; the actions of the buddhas prove it. They need food – it does not grow inside. They need water – they have to seek, and find it outside. And still they go on saying, "All that is outside is illusory."

And the Zorbas, although they say that they are only living on the outside, are simply unreasonable – because the outside can exist only if there is an inside. They are inseparable. Have you seen anything which has only outside and no inside? Have you seen a coin which has only one side? Howsoever thin you make it, both sides remain together.

The first step to understand is: the most significant approach is to relax and be in love with your body, with your heart. Don't create any conflict, bring them closer – because centuries have made them so unbridgeable. And as they come closer and become one you will not be just a Zorba or just a buddha, you will be Zorba the Buddha. You will be a total man. And in your totality is beauty, is bliss, is truth.

Your reason and your passion are the rudder and the sails of your seafaring soul.

When you have understood their unity and they are no longer in conflict, suddenly you will see a new space arising in you, you will see your soul. Now that there is no conflict in your body, your reason, your heart, you have time, silence and space to see something of the beyond – the soul.

You are basically a triangle: reason, heart and soul. But very few people have reached to the soul, because the battlefield continues. You don't have any time to explore – the Zorba goes on pulling you outside, and the buddha goes on pulling you inside. It is a strange struggle that has been imposed on you by all those who want you to be weak, who want you to be without souls – just machines, robots.

He is saying: *Your reason and your passion are the rudder and the sails of your seafaring soul. If either your sails or your rudder be broken, you can but toss and drift* – and that is what almost all of humanity is doing, tossing and drifting – *or else be held at a standstill in mid-seas.* That is a kind of death before death.

For reason, ruling alone, is a force confining...

Reason has its limits. It cannot accept that which is limitless.

And passion unattended is a flame that burns to its own destruction.

Your passion is your fire – the fire of your life. But unattended, unlistened to, ignored, the fire is going to destroy itself. The same fire could be used by reason to destroy the limits, to burn the limited imprisonment, and you would have the whole sky for yourself.

Therefore let your soul exalt your reason to the height of passion...

Passion knows no limits. Your energy is a source inexhaustible, because your energy is the energy of the whole universe.

...let your soul exalt your reason to the height of passion, that it may sing.

Blessed is the man whose reason starts singing and dancing, because reason knows only curiosity, doubt, questioning; it does not know anything about singing, dancing, celebrating – those belong to your heart. But if your soul, your awareness, brings them together, they will become partners in a dance, partners in a song so deeply in tune that all their duality disappears.

To me, this disappearance of duality is the beginning of a new life without any conflict, without any battlefield. Your life starts to become the Garden of Eden. All your energies are enough to create a paradise within you.

It has been told to you that if you follow certain conditions as a Christian, a Hindu or a Mohammedan, you will enter into paradise. But I say to you: you never enter paradise. It is paradise which enters you the moment the battlefield has disappeared and your heart and your reason are dancing in tune. Paradise is waiting for the moment when it can enter. In this joy, silence and peace, paradise has to come to you.

The whole idea of you going to paradise is nonsense. There is no paradise outside you, and there is no hell outside you. You are living in hell when you are in conflict, fighting with yourself. And heaven is in you when there is absolute silence, and a song arises in your being of totality, of organic unity.

And let it direct your passion with reason, that your passion may live through its own daily resurrection...

Never forget what Kahlil Gibran is saying, because these are not only words, they are seeds which can transform you into a beautiful garden where birds will start singing, flowers will start opening and paradise is waiting for that moment to knock on your doors: "I have come, you are ready."

What he is saying is, the first thing is that reason should be raised by you, your awareness, to the height of passion *that it may sing.* And the second thing is more important:

And let it direct your passion with reason...

...so that you are not lost in a blind groping. On the heights, having no eyes is very dangerous – then it is better to remain in the valley with all other blind people. Even if you fall, you will not die – maybe a scratch, or maybe a fracture, but not death.

Let reason direct your passion, let it become the eyes of your heart, and then you will come to know why Christians say that after the crucifixion there was resurrection. It may not be – perhaps it is not a historical fact – but it has a deep psychological and spiritual depth.

Each moment your passion dies, because passion knows nothing of the past and nothing of the future; those are the accumulations of reason. Passion knows only this moment – each moment it dies, and if directed with the eyes of reason, each moment there will be a resurrection. It will die and it will be reborn fresher, younger, better, more refined.

...and like the phoenix rise above its own ashes.

The mythological bird, the phoenix, is really a way of telling you that you should learn to die each moment and be born again each moment. Your life should be a continuous death and a continuous resurrection so that you remain fresh to the very last breath; otherwise dust goes on gathering, and you die almost thirty, forty years before people understand, "This fellow is dead."

The hippies used to say, "Never believe a man who has passed the age of thirty" – because at the age of almost thirty or nearabout a person dies, and then he lives for forty years, fifty years, a posthumous life, because resurrection does not happen.

But hippies were only a reaction – that is why you don't find any old hippies. They had all died at the age of thirty; now they are living their posthumous lives in the marketplace very efficiently. They have forgotten all about it, it was just a dream that every young man has to pass through; now they laugh about it – it is nothing but a fading memory.

I have been in search of an old hippie – I have not been successful. Old hippies don't exist, for the simple reason that they don't know it is not a question of reacting against the society, it is a question of inner transformation, of learning the alchemy of how to die peacefully and allow the energy to resurrect, just like the phoenix bird, on its own ashes.

That is one of the most powerful and meaningful metaphors. I have not come across another metaphor that is so significant and so strong. It is the whole philosophy of religion: dying and being reborn you remain always fresh, you remain always in a flow; you don't just grow old, you grow up.

Growing old is not a great quality – all animals grow old, all trees grow old. Only man has the privilege, the prerogative, that he can grow up and can remain as fresh and young, even in old age, as he was when he was under the age of thirty. Full of dreams of the beyond, even on the deathbed he is not sad that he is going to leave this earth; on the contrary, he is immensely excited about the new pilgrimage that is going to start, because he knows that no death is a death – every death is a resurrection too.

This becomes a truth only when your reason and your passion are together, when your Zorba and buddha are not fighting, but hugging each other.

> *I would have you consider your judgment and your appetite even as you would two loved guests in your house.*
> *Surely you would not honor one guest above the other; for he who is more mindful of one loses the love and the faith of both.*

I have heard about a man who was in love with two women. Both women wanted assurance, security, "Be honest and say whom you are going to marry." And it was difficult for the poor man, because the woman who was very beautiful was very poor, and the woman who was just homely was immensely rich, and all those riches were going to be his. You can understand his dilemma.

They had gone in a boat just to enjoy the sea and the sun. Suddenly the rich woman told him, "Stop the boat here in the middle of the ocean. I cannot wait anymore. You have to make the decision. Tell us whom you love!"

The man must have been very intelligent. He said, "What kind of question are you asking? I love each of you more than the other." And both the women were immensely satisfied.

Among the hills, when you sit in the cool shade of the white poplars, sharing the peace and serenity of distant fields and meadows – then let your heart say in silence, "God rests in reason." And when the storm comes, and the mighty wind shakes the forest, and thunder and lightning proclaim the majesty of the sky, – then let your heart say in awe, "God moves in passion."
And since you are a breath in God's sphere, and a leaf in God's forest, you too should rest in reason and move in passion.

This is the greatest synthesis which man needs – and needs immediately – because the whole humanity of the past has missed this synthesis, this synchronicity. But I want my people to enjoy God in every possible situation – when it is day, God is light, and when it is night, God is darkness. Don't create any conflict.

Once you are no longer a battlefield you have become a temple – and you are not going to purchase a statue of God to enshrine in the temple. Living godliness has always entered the being of the man who has turned into a holy place, who has become sacred.

You have all the elements that are needed. You have all the possibilities that are required. If you miss, nobody else will be responsible for it except you.

God is just waiting at the door, but you are in such a mess, who would like to enter inside? And even if he knocks on your door, you cannot listen. There is so much going on, so much fight, that you are not going to listen to the small knock on the door. And there is no strong electric button on your door that God can go on pushing. He still uses the old human way of knocking with his own hand. That gives him the idea whether you are prepared or not, whether you are ready to receive him or not: have you become a host that he can become a guest?

9

FRIENDSHIP
from friendship to friendliness

And a youth said, Speak to us of Friendship.
And he answered, saying:
Your friend is your needs answered.
He is your field which you sow with love and reap with
thanksgiving.
And he is your board and your fireside.
For you come to him with your hunger, and you seek him for
peace.

When your friend speaks his mind you fear not the "nay" in your
own mind, nor do you withhold the "ay."
And when he is silent your heart ceases not to listen to his heart;
For without words, in friendship, all thoughts, all desires, all
expectations are born and shared, with joy that is unacclaimed.
When you part from your friend, you grieve not;
For that which you love most in him may be clearer in his absence,
as the mountain to the climber is clearer from the plain.
And let there be no purpose in friendship save the deepening of the
spirit.
For love that seeks aught but the disclosure of its own mystery is

not love but a net cast forth: and only the unprofitable is caught.

And let your best be for your friend.
If he must know the ebb of your tide, let him know its flood also.
For what is your friend that you should seek him with hours to kill?
Seek him always with hours to live.
For it is his to fill your need, but not your emptiness.
And in the sweetness of friendship let there be laughter, and sharing of pleasures.
For in the dew of little things the heart finds its morning and is refreshed.

M y eyes become full of tears when I see that Kahlil Gibran is only sometimes a vehicle of godliness, of truth – but not always.

I would have loved him to be always on the sunlit peaks of consciousness, but he goes on down into the valleys, which are dark. Although his articulateness remains the same, and his poetry carries the same beauty, the truth is lost. He is so articulate, that unless you know the truth you will not be able to make any distinction where he falls down and where he rises to the highest peaks.

His Zorba and his buddha are not together; they are not yet an organic unity. So when Zorba speaks, of course the language is the same as that of buddha, but the meaning is not of buddha. It seems he has a split personality and I feel tears for him, that a man of such great genius could not manage to become one, he remained two – just as every ordinary man is.

Kahlil Gibran is not enlightened; hence he cannot see the bird's-eye view of the whole. But because he has great intelligence he manages, whenever he is falling down, to make his words hide his fall. I love the man, because it is very rare to find such a man, but I feel sorry for him too because he could not become integrated, crystallized. You will not be able to find out when he is flying high like an eagle and when he is just walking on the earth amongst you; you will not be able to recognize him. That's very unfortunate.

We have missed another Gautam Buddha for the simple reason that he was praised all over the world by those who knew nothing of the organic unity. He himself cannot see the contradictions; and neither will you be able to see the contradictions. But I want to be honest and sincere because I love him, and love is a fire; it burns all that is false and saves only that which is true.

And a youth said, Speak to us of Friendship.

The very word *friendship* is not of the heights – the word *friendliness* rises to the moon, to the sun – because the word *friendship* is just of the mind. It is confining; you can be in friendship with only a few people. But friendliness is vast; you can be friendly to the trees, to the mountains, to the stars.

Friendship is hiding a bondage too. All words like *relationship*, *friendship*, are superficial. *Lovingness*, *friendliness*, have a totally different meaning. When you are talking about friendship it is a very small thing – a kind of bondage and dependence on the person with whom you feel the friendship.

But friendliness is freedom – you are not dependent on anybody. Friendship is objective, and friendliness is your love shared unconditionally with the whole existence. They don't mean the same thing. Friendship can become any moment its opposite; the so-called friend can turn into your enemy. But friendliness has no particular address. It is not for anybody, it is for the whole existence. It can never turn into its opposite.

Remember, that which can turn into its opposite very easily – and you know friends become enemies, enemies become friends – is very superficial, a false substitute. But friendliness is not addressed to anyone; it is the love overflowing within you, unconditionally. There is no possibility of it turning bitter – you are the master of it. In friendship you are not the master. Friendship is like marriage, an artificial thing, but friendliness is your very nature.

And a youth said, Speak to us of Friendship.
And he answered, saying:
Your friend is your needs answered.

This is an ugly statement, but it is a logical consequence because he has not changed the basic question. He should have told the youth that friendship is worthless; friendliness is invaluable. *Your friend is your needs answered.* I say it again: it is ugly, because friendship is demanding.

Friendliness simply gives its fragrance to all without any exception – and it is fulfilled in giving it. It is not a need; it is an overflowing love. You can be friendly with the trees, you can be friendly with the stars, but there is no demand, no condition. Of course your needs will be fulfilled, but not because you have been demanding. Your friendliness will bring you tremendous treasures. Make a clear distinction between these two words.

Friendship is a prison. Friendliness is absolute freedom: you give out of your abundance; it is not a need. Of course, existence understands that the person who is giving without any demands is a rare being. Existence takes care of your needs, but they are not demanded. Even if it does not fulfill your needs, it simply shows that deep down in your unconscious you are clinging to the idea of friendship. Only fools can be deceived just by changing the words.

Existence is so abundant; just don't ask.

Because Kahlil Gibran remained a Christian... Although he was a great intellectual, he was not a meditator. He is repeating Jesus Christ in different words; Jesus says, "Ask and it shall be given." He reduces you into a beggar. I say unto you, "Never ask and you will receive it. Ask and you are not going to get it." Your very asking is ugly.

Jesus says, "Seek and you will find." I say to you, "Just be silent, a nobody, and existence will pour into you from all directions" – because the man who seeks is still seeking decorations for his ego, and existence does not understand the language of ego. No tree is an egoist, no mountain is an egoist, no bird is an egoist, but existence goes on and on giving them all that they need or even more than they need.

Jesus says, "Knock and the door shall be opened." These are superficial statements, because I know there is no door where you can knock. God is all over the place. Don't knock – that is violence. Just wait.

Your waiting – you will be mature in your waiting. You will become capable of receiving, open. God always comes as a gift. God always comes to the emperors, not to the beggars. You need not go to God – and even if you want to, where are you going to find him? He can find you because he is the whole.

Neither ask nor seek nor knock on the door – trust. If you are worthy, ripe, the spring is bound to come with thousands of flowers in your being.

Your friend is your needs answered. The statement is Jewish, business-like. Love is not a business. Love is the song of your soul. Friendship is the fragrance of that love, and winds will carry it over the seas, over the mountains to the faraway stars.

Love is not getting. Love is giving – and so is friendliness.

He is your field which you sow with love and reap with thanksgiving.

Sounds good; Kahlil Gibran is a genius in finding beautiful words, but he knows nothing. Even behind his beautiful words and poetry there is darkness, unconsciousness. *He is your field...* A friend is your field? You are going to exploit the field by sowing with love? It does not matter: your love is not for the friend, your love is for reaping the crop.

And reap with thanksgiving. It will be very strange to you that friends are one soul in two bodies. There is no question of thanksgiving, it is understood in silence. It is not the ugly "thank you" which is just a formality. And, *sow with love...* You are going to exploit the friend. How can you sow with love? Your love is a facade, a bribe, a persuasion. Because of your love the friend will become a field for you. But your real interest is sowing the seeds and reaping the crop, and your thanksgiving is empty. If the friend has not given you anything, your thanksgiving will disappear.

Hence I say to you: give, share with love, with no desire in your heart lurking anywhere for return, and the question of thanksgiving then takes a new dimension. You are thankful that the friend received your love, received your songs, received your abundance.

You should be thankful, not because you have received from the friend; you should be thankful that he has not rejected you. He had every right to reject. He was humble and he was understanding. Feel grateful, but for a totally different reason.

And he is your board and your fireside.

What nonsense is he talking about? It hurts me because he is a very sensitive man. *And he is your board and your fireside* – your friend? *You* should be a board for your friend and *you* should be a fireside for your friend. That is the difference between friendship and friendliness. I can forgive the youth who asked the question, but I cannot forgive Kahlil Gibran who is giving the answer.

When your friend speaks his mind you fear not the "nay" in your mind, nor do you withhold the "ay."

Why should one be afraid of a friend? – then what are you going to do with an enemy? So when the friend speaks his mind, don't be afraid to say no, because he will understand. And, *nor do you withhold the "ay."*

What *is* friendliness? If you cannot expose your heart, naked, in friendliness, then you are a cunning businessman. You think of profit, you think of future, you think of the response. Although you are feeling to say no, you are afraid that the friendship will be destroyed by your no. And he is your need, he is your board, he is your field – are you a cannibal?

It shows the secrets of a cunning mind: Say yes when you know that he will be happy, say no only when you are certain that he will be happy. You are not being honest, straightforward. If you cannot be honest with a friend, with whom are you going to be honest? That's why I say friendliness is a far greater and higher value. It can say no without any fear, because it knows the friend will understand, and he will be grateful to you that you were not deceiving him.

Friendliness means standing exposed to each other, because you have trust. Friendship is a very poor thing.

And when he is silent your heart ceases not to listen to his heart.

This is the split personality of Kahlil Gibran. In the very invention of Almustafa he is being political. He is not speaking directly, he is speaking through Almustafa because Almustafa is only a fiction. But it is a good security: people will take it as poetry, a fiction, beautiful.

He has been praised all over the world for this small book, *The Prophet*. Perhaps I am the first one who is trying to shift and create a clear-cut division between when he is honest and when he is not honest.

And without words, in friendship, all thoughts, all desires...

He never goes beyond the mind. Friendliness is beyond the mind, just as love is beyond the mind; in fact, friendliness rises higher even than love.

In the Upanishads there is a tremendous statement. It has been a tradition in the East that when somebody gets married he goes with his wife to a seer, to a sage, for his blessings. And such a strange blessing does not exist anywhere in any literature, in any tradition.

The sage, the man of enlightenment, blesses them with the words, "You should give birth to ten children, and after that your husband will be your eleventh child." It looks absurd, the husband is going to be the eleventh child? – but it has such a profundity. You have loved enough, you have given birth to ten children; now it is time to rise above love itself. Even your husband is your eleventh child. Go beyond love, and merge and melt into friendship. Refine it to the point where it becomes friendliness; then neither are you a wife nor is the husband a husband, but you are two souls living together in friendliness.

...all expectations are born and shared, with joy that is unacclaimed.

Love or friendliness have no expectations. That is the beauty of friendliness – you don't expect anything, because wherever there is expectation, just behind it, like a shadow, is frustration. And you cannot dictate to the future; you don't even know what the future is going to be.

When I was a postgraduate in the university, a very beautiful girl was also studying the same subjects as me. For two years we remained studying the same subjects – philosophy, religion and psychology – and then finally we had to depart. She was a rich girl, the daughter of the collector of the city. I had gone out, her car was waiting – and perhaps she was also waiting; there was no need for her to sit inside the car and wait. It took two years for her to say to me, "I have been very much frustrated. I wanted you to say to me, 'I love you.'"

I said, "Love is not an expectation; and if it is an expectation, frustration is bound to happen." Why does the whole world look so frustrated? – for the simple reason that you have so many expectations. I told the girl, "What you are saying today you should have told me the first time you started feeling love toward me."

She said, "The gone is gone; we cannot go back to the past. But this is my last day in the city. I was staying here with my father because he is the collector, but my whole family lives in New Delhi. By the evening I will be gone. So I gathered courage and asked you. I love you. Can you not promise me that whenever you will love I should be given the priority?"

I said, "I cannot promise about the future – the future is absolutely unknown. I cannot even promise for tomorrow or the next moment."

To me, promising shows the retardedness of the mind. Every promise is going to be a trouble because you are unaware of a simple fact: the future is absolutely unknown.

Where you will land tomorrow nobody knows. Any promise is irreligious, because it shows a stupid mind that cannot understand the future. A religious person can neither expect, because that is concerned with the future; nor can he promise, because that too is concerned with the future. The religious person lives in the moment. But he says, "When expectations from your friend..."

When you part from your friend, you grieve not;
For that which you love most in him may be clearer in his absence...

There is some truth in it. Human mind is such that we start taking everything for granted, so only in absence do we become aware that it was our foolishness to take something for granted.

We live our whole lives without friendliness, without love, because we had taken it for granted: "It is always somebody else who dies; I'm always alive." So you can postpone living. And everybody is postponing living, not knowing what the future contains for you.

I again insist and emphasize: don't take anything for granted. Live in the moment. And living in the moment will give you the strength to live in any other moments – if there is going to be a future. Your strength will go on growing. Otherwise... It is sad that there are many people who, when they are dying, realize for the first time, "My God, I was alive for seventy years but I went on postponing. And now there is no future to postpone to."

Never give any promises, because you may not be able to fulfill them. Make it clear, "I am not the owner of the future." But there are people who are promising about everything. To their lovers they are saying, "I will love you forever." These are the promises that become their imprisonments.

Say to your friends, to your lovers, "Only one moment is given to me at a time; not even two moments are given together. So this moment I can say absolutely that I love you, but for tomorrow it is impossible to say that I will love you. Yesterday I was not in love with you. Tomorrow perhaps the fragrance of love, just as it came without any advance notice, may leave. Then I will be in bondage to my own promise, ashamed of my own words."

Promising, keeping your word – the whole of humanity has imprisoned itself. Live, and live totally, but *now* – because that is all that you have, for certain, in your hand. But I know the stupid minds of people. If you say to a woman, "I promise that I will love you this moment, but I cannot say about the next moment. Neither do I want any expectations from you, nor will I give any expectations to you; otherwise life is going to be a continual frustration…"

And let there be no purpose in friendship…

That is the strangeness of Kahlil Gibran, his split personality. He has to be sorted out – when he starts speaking as a Zorba, and when he starts speaking as a buddha. He was never able to come to a synthesis between the two – the lowest and the highest.

And let there be no purpose…save the deepening of the spirit.

But that too is a purpose. Sometimes people who have such clear eyes about everything in the world are absolutely unconscious about what they are saying. First he says: *And let there be no purpose in friendship save the deepening of the spirit* – but that too is a purpose. In fact if there is no purpose, the deepening of the spirit will happen of its own accord. It need not be mentioned; otherwise the sentence becomes contradictory. The first part and the second part are contradictory.

First he says: *Your friend is your needs answered,* and now he says, "There should be no purpose in friendship." But what are your needs except purposes? Every purpose destroys the beauty of friendliness.

Friendliness should have no purposes, no needs – although this is a miracle of life, that if you have no purposes, no needs, your needs will be fulfilled, your purposes will be fulfilled. But that should not be in your mind; otherwise you don't have the friendliness, you don't have love.

For love that seeks aught but the disclosure of its own mystery is not love but a net cast forth: and only the unprofitable is caught.

Love that seeks aught but the disclosure of its own mystery is not love, because love is a mystery, and there is no way to make it open.

Love is like the roots of the trees, hidden deep in the earth. Share the fragrance, the flowers, the foliage, the greenery, but don't try to pull out the tree to see from where it is getting so many colors, so much fragrance, so much beauty, because that will be the death of the tree. The roots have to remain hidden, secret, a mystery – not that you want... But you cannot go against the laws of nature.

Share your fragrance, share your flowers. Dance in the moon, in the wind, in the rain. Have you seen this morning? – all the trees were so happy, dancing in the rain, throwing all the dust away, becoming fresh and young again. But the roots have to remain mysterious. Once you expose the roots, love is going to die. And it is unfortunate that every lover, every friend, is very curious to know your mystery, to know your secret. Lovers are continually fighting, saying, "You are hiding something."

Thousands of years, and man has come to conclude that it is impossible to understand the mystery of a woman, because she has deeper roots in the earth. Men's eyes are fixed toward the sky. It is idiotic – the effort to reach the moon. Now the effort is to reach Mars!

You are not able to live on this beautiful earth with peace and silence, with love, without boundaries of nations, without discrimi- nations of color, without making half of the humanity – the woman – just a purchased prostitute, a life-long prostitute. You have not been able to figure out how to live on the earth, and your eyes are fixed on the moon.

Do you know that in English there is a word, *lunatic?* It comes from the root *lunar. Lunar* means "the moon." Man is a lunatic. In fact, to try to find out the mystery of your lover is being just as ugly as all Peeping Toms are. Nature does not want you to be de-mystified, because it is in mystery that love blossoms, friendliness dances.

It is good that neither men understand women, nor women understand men. There is no need for knowledgeability. What is needed is enough space for each other, so that your secrets and your mysteries remain hidden. It is because of that mystery that you have fallen in love. If you demystify the woman, the love may also disappear.

Knowledge is so meaningless, and mystery is so profound. Wonder about the mystery, but never question what it is; your friendliness, your love will know no bounds. The closer you will be, the more the mystery will go on deepening.

But Kahlil Gibran seems to be continually confused – and it is natural. Sometimes there are glimpses when he says tremendous truths, and sometimes there are moments when he falls back into darkness and starts talking like an idiot. In all the statements you can see it.

First he says your friend is your needs answered, and second he says, there should be no purpose. What are the needs if not purposes? And immediately he says, makes an exception, that the deepening of your soul should be your only purpose. In existence, in reality, there are no exceptions.

And look again – *but a net cast forth: and only the unprofitable is caught.* Purpose should not be there except the deepening of the soul – which is a by-product. And again he forgets what he is saying. *Unprofitable* – now it becomes almost the language of the businessman, not of a poet, because the unprofitable takes you to the higher realms of being. The profitable drags you down to the gravitation of the earth.

And let your best be for your friend.

He walks in a zigzag. I am not condemning him, I am simply making it clear that a man of his genius cannot see simple things in one statement. *And let your best be for your friend* – but tastes differ. What is best for you may be worthless for your friend. Who are you to decide what is best for him? I will not say that. I will say, "Open your heart and allow the friend; whatsoever he chooses is his."

If he must know the ebb of your tide, let him know its flood also.

That is just a truism. You should open your heart totally. Ebbs or tides, all should be available for the friend.

For what is your friend that you should seek him with hours to kill?

All friends are doing that – they are killing each others' hours because they are both empty, and they don't know how to be alone, how to enjoy being alone.

Seek him always with hours to live.

Not to kill time, but with hours to live. This is great, glorious. But he seems to be like a pendulum of a clock that goes on moving from one extreme to the other. Certainly he is not a man of awareness; although a man of immense capacity to express – a man who can express with golden words.

Seek him always with hours to live.
For it is his to fill your need, but not your emptiness.

Do you understand what I am saying – the pendulum? But Kahlil Gibran himself is not aware that one statement immediately contradicts the other statement. *For it is his to fill your need* – what happened about expectations? What happened about profit? He has forgotten, it seems, *but not your emptiness.* This is something to be understood – that man's greatest need is not to be empty, not to be dark, not to be alone. His greatest need is to be needed. If nobody needs him he becomes more and more aware of his emptiness.

So, even this single sentence is contradictory. For it is his will... *For it is his to fill your need* – but is not emptiness your greatest need? For what are you continually engaged? – just so that you don't feel empty. You *are* empty.

The East has a far more profound answer: that the emptiness need not be negative. Don't fill it with all kinds of rubbish. Emptiness can become your temple filled with godliness. Still it will be empty, because godliness is only a quality. Fill it with light – still it will be empty. Fill it with silence. Transform the negative emptiness into a positive phenomenon, and you have done a miracle to yourself.

*And in the knowledge of friendship let there be laughter, and
sharing of pleasures.*

Kahlil Gibran, again and again, goes on saying things without
giving you the key to how it is possible. Any idiot can come and say,
"Fill your garden with greenery, with roseflowers, with ponds, with
beautiful lotuses," but this is not enough. You are talking to a man
who has never known greenness, who has never known roses, who
has never known lotuses, and who is absolutely unaware of how he
is going to do it. The key is missing.

This is not only with Kahlil Gibran; almost all the religions of the
world are in the same boat. They say, "You should not be angry."
But what is the way? Anger is there! "You should not be jealous." But
what is the way to get rid of jealousy? "You should not be competitive." Bogus commandments!

It is beautiful to be silent, but where is the meditation that brings
silence to you? "You should not be jealous" – but where is the understanding that in jealousy you are burning your own heart? It does
not harm anybody but yourself.

How can you get rid of competitiveness – because they all are
teaching, "Don't be competitive," and on the other hand, "Be something." They are giving ideals to you: "Be a Jesus." But there are
millions of Christians. You will have to compete. They are saying,
"Don't be jealous," but they are forcing people to be jealous, tying one
man to one woman. When the love disappears and the spring is gone,
then the man starts finding backdoor ways – and the woman too.

I have heard...

There was a case in the court. The husband and wife wanted a
divorce. The story must be old – divorce was almost impossible,
immoral, unvirtuous. The magistrate said, "Love each other. Remain
together until death separates you."

The woman asked, "You are giving good advice, but how to love
a man whom I simply hate? And I also know he cannot love me; he
also hates me. So please give us some method so that the hate disappears and is transformed into love."

The man said, "My God, I don't know anything about it. But you
will have to take an oath that you will make every effort to remain
together. Don't create a precedent of immorality in the society."

The woman said, "I am ready to take the oath, putting my hand on my son's head."

It was a strange scene, because the judge became fidgety. He said, "No, not on your son. Just use your religious book."

The woman said, "I am a mother, and to be motherly is my religion. But why are you looking so fidgety? Do you want me to expose you before the court? – because the son is yours!"

What a hypocritical society we are living in. The magistrate is trying to rule that they should live together, and the magistrate is a secret lover of the woman. Not only that, even the child is his, not of the husband of the woman. That's why he is afraid.

She said, "Now do you understand? You are unfaithful to your wife. This son is your son, I am only his mother. My husband has his own relationships – and you will be surprised: it is your wife! And the children that you think are yours are not yours."

It is such a hypocritical society. We go on and on living in misery, in untruth – even in our courts.

Once I was in a court in Jabalpur. There was a church, a very beautiful church. But when the British government left in 1947, all the worshippers of the church also left for their country. The church had remained locked for almost ten years. It has a beautiful garden, which was completely destroyed. The church belongs to the Church of England, it is their property.

I had a few friends who were Christians and I said, "You are idiots. Your Christ has been in imprisonment, not in a church, for ten years, and perhaps he is going to be there for his whole life. Gather a few young Christians." They were very much afraid because the property belonged to the Church of England. I said, "Don't be bothered. I will inaugurate the church. Just clean it, renovate it, throw out all those locks, break them. The church belongs to those who worship there. It is not property. You worship there so it is *your* church."

They said, "You are creating trouble. Soon there will be a case in the court."

I said, "Don't be worried. I will fight with you. You can tell the court the truth – that it was I who had told you to."

It was so reasonable, so they somehow – but reluctantly, wishy-washy – managed to break the locks, renovate the church and clean the garden. And on one Sunday I inaugurated it.

Immediately other Christians informed the Church of England, "This is trespass. Not only trespass, these people have taken the property." And it was a big property, almost twenty acres of land, and the church was very beautiful.

The Church of England had its representative bishop in Nagpur. In those days Nagpur used to be the capital of Madhya Pradesh. So he informed them, "Drag all those people" – particularly me, because I am not even a Christian – "to the court."

Standing in the witness box I asked the magistrate, "Before I take the oath for truth, a few things have to be cleared that, after taking the oath, will be impossible to clear."

He said, "This is a strange thing. First the oath has to be taken."

I said, "The things that I am going to say to you are about the oath, so why should I not be allowed to say some things before?"

He said, "Okay, you can say it, but it is not the routine way."

I said, "The first thing is: I have seen you visiting prostitutes, and the whole city knows you are a homosexual; hence I don't have any respect for you. I can say to a donkey, 'Honorable sir,' but I cannot say to you truthfully, 'Honorable sir,' because that will be a lie. My heart will not be with it. So allow me, if you insist on the oath, to say what my heart says is true; otherwise drop the idea of the oath. Secondly, I want to know on what I should take the oath."

He said, "You can take oath on the Bible, the Hindu Gita, or any religious book."

I said, "They are all full of lies. Have you ever looked into them? And this is such an absurdity – that an oath for truth has to be taken holding a book which is full of lies.

"And thirdly: the very idea of an oath is repugnant to me, because by implication I am accepting that without an oath I am going to lie, that only under oath will I be saying the truth. I cannot accept this condemnation of me. I speak the truth as I feel it in my own being, and these rotten books, thousands of years old... I have no respect for these books either. Only people like you can have faith in these obscene – but called holy – books. But I am ready to do any formality.

"Just remember: once I have taken an oath holding a holy book which is full of lies I will be continually lying. I have to follow the book. First, prove that these books consist of truth, first prove that you are worthy of being called 'Honorable sir,' and first convince me that the very concept of oath is not ugly.

"It means my whole life I have been lying – only under oath can I speak the truth. And you are an intelligent man; you can see that if a man can lie his whole life, his oath can also be a lie. Who can prevent me?"

I said, "I don't belong to any religion, I don't belong to any superstition – so it is up to you."

He immediately said, "Call the second witness."

I said, "Not yet, because I still have one point to make. A temple belongs to those who worship there. A temple is not just a piece of land, is not a house. It cannot be owned by anybody. The Church of England has no right to own the church. The church belongs to those who pray there, meditate there; they are the real owners."

He was trembling. He said, "I have heard you, but you have raised such fundamental questions that it is better... Call the second witness!"

This world is so full of hypocrisy. Your leaders are continually lying. Nobody is allowed to live, but to lie...

And in the sweetness of friendship let there be laughter, and sharing of pleasures.

But how? You have destroyed man's capacity even to smile. And if you want – the idea is good – then tell people how they can resurrect their life, their laughter, their dancing, their sharing of pleasures. All the religions are against pleasures. No religion has talked about sharing but, "Give to the poor, because in return you will receive one-thousandfold more after death." This is pure business! In fact, even to call it business is wrong; it is gambling. No church, no synagogue, no temple would allow people to laugh, to dance, to sing. You have crushed man's spirit so completely that he is almost a corpse.

The trouble with Kahlil Gibran is that he is a great intellectual power; all these statements he is making through his reason, but not through his experience. If he was talking through his own experience he would have given the keys – how to undo all that centuries have done to man.

For in the dew of little things the heart finds its morning and is refreshed.

He writes beautiful words – but of what use? The highest evolved being on the earth cannot laugh. All the religions have been teaching, "Renounce the world." You should have contradicted that if you want...

For in the dew of little things the heart finds its morning and is refreshed. No religion allows you pleasure; no religion allows you laughter; no religion allows you to enjoy the little things of life. On the contrary, they condemn every little thing – small things. And life consists of small things.

Religions talk about God, but not about flowers; they talk about paradise, but not about nourishing food; they talk about all kinds of pleasures in heaven, but not on the earth. The earth is a punishment. You have been thrown to earth the way somebody is thrown into a jail.

Kahlil Gibran is great in his words, but something of the coward is present in his unconscious, otherwise he should have also added, "Those who are teaching otherwise are not your friends, they are your enemies. All religions are enemies of man, all priests are enemies of man, all governments are enemies of man." But you will not find a single sentence like that. That's why he is respected all over the world – because he has not annoyed anybody. I am saying the same things, but filling the gaps that he has left out, changing the words that he is unaware of.

He is a beautiful man, but not courageous. He is still a sheep, not a shepherd; a sheep, not a lion. He should have roared like a lion – because he had the capacity. But a great man has died without even getting his books listed by the Polack pope on his black list – that no Catholic should read these books.

All my books are on the black list. To read them is a direct and short-cut way to go to hell. In fact, I am perfectly happy that you will all be with me in hell. We will transform it into heaven. And one day you will find God knocking on the door, saying, "Please let me in. I am bored and tired of all kinds of idiots."

10

PLEASURE
the seed of blissfulness

Then a hermit, who visited the city once a year, came forth and said, Speak to us of Pleasure.
And he answered, saying:
Pleasure is a freedom-song,
But it is not freedom.
It is the blossoming of your desires,
But it is not their fruit.
It is a depth calling unto a height,
But it is not the deep nor the high.
It is the caged taking wing,
But it is not space encompassed.
Ay, in very truth, pleasure is a freedom-song.
And I fain would have you sing it with fullness of heart; yet I would not have you lose your hearts in the singing.

Some of your youth seek pleasure as if it were all, and they are judged and rebuked.
I would not judge nor rebuke them. I would have them seek.
For they shall find pleasure, but not her alone;

Seven are her sisters, and the least of them is more beautiful than pleasure.
Have you not heard of the man who was digging in the earth for roots and found a treasure?

Kahlil Gibran has posed every question in its right context. It is not a question coming out of the blue, it is a question representing the questioner. And he has made every effort to answer the questioner by answering his question. These are two different things.

The philosophical approach toward life only answers the question; it does not matter who is asking, the question in itself is important to the philosopher. But to the mystic, the question is only the beginning of a deep exposure of the questioner; hence, the real answer is not arrowed toward the question, but toward the questioner. The question has its roots in the heart of the one who has asked, and unless you answer him, you have not answered.

And Kahlil Gibran is very careful that, when he is answering the question, he should not forget the questioner. The question is superficial; the real problem is deep down in the heart of one who has asked.

Then a hermit, who visited the city once a year, came forth and said, Speak to us of Pleasure.

Does it not look very strange that a hermit should ask about pleasure? It appears so, but in truth the hermit has renounced pleasure and is tortured by his own renunciation. He cannot forget the possibility that perhaps those who are living the life of pleasure are the right ones, perhaps by renouncing life and its pleasures he has simply gone wrong.

And the feeling is not just a superficial thought, it is deep in his very being because since he has renounced pleasure, he has lost all zest for life, all will even to breathe. Even to wake up in the morning – for what? Since he has renounced he has died a kind of death; he is no longer a living being, although he breathes, eats, walks, speaks. But I say unto you: his life is only posthumous. He is like a ghost who has died long before. The moment he renounced existence he renounced life also; he committed a spiritual suicide.

But all the religions have been teaching nothing but spiritual suicide. They are all anti-life – and if you are anti-life, naturally the only way for you is to go on repressing your natural desires, longings.

The hermit, who has been praised down the ages as saint, as holy, is nothing but a repressed soul who has not allowed himself to live, who has not allowed himself to dance, to love. He is like a tree which has renounced its own foliage, which has renounced its own flowers, and its own fruits. Dry and juiceless the tree stands, just a faded memory.

All this has been done because there are vested interests in the world which want you to be just alive, but not to live; just to survive, but not in your fullness – only at the minimum, not at the maximum. They have turned every human being into a summertime river. They don't allow you to be flooded with rain and to have a taste of something widening, expanding – some dream of a future meeting with the ocean. A summertime river has shrunken, has become shallow, has become broken.

The hermit has died at the very center of his being. His body goes on living, but he does not know what life is, because pleasure is the only language that life understands. Although pleasure is not the end, it is certainly the beginning – and you cannot reach the end if you have missed the beginning. The hermit needs all your compassion, not your worship. Your worship has been the cause of many people committing suicide, because you have been worshipping those who are renouncing pleasure. You are fulfilling their egos and destroying their souls. You are partners in a great crime: they are committing suicide, but you are also murdering them by your worship.

The question – coming from a hermit asking Almustafa, *Speak to us of Pleasure* – is immensely significant. It needs courage even to ask such a question, as far as your so-called sages and saints are concerned.

It must have been twenty-five years ago, when I happened to speak in a conference... Just before me a Jaina monk, Chandan Muni, who was very much respected by his community and religion, inaugurated the conference. He spoke about great blissfulness, great joy in renouncing life, in renouncing the mundane, profane pleasures. I was sitting by his side, watching him, but I could not see any sign that he had known what he was talking about. He appeared dry and dead, his statements were repetitions, parrot-like, from the scriptures. It was not a poetry – spontaneous, flowing like a stream from the mountains, young, fresh, singing, dancing toward the ocean.

When I spoke after him, I said, "The man who was speaking just now is simply a hypocrite" – and he was sitting by my side – "he knows nothing of ecstasy, nothing of blissfulness, because the man who has renounced pleasure has renounced the first step which leads to the final step of blissfulness. It is impossible to reach to blissfulness if you are against pleasure and against life."

There was a great shock, because people don't speak what they feel; people speak only what other people appreciate. And I could feel the vibrations of Chandan Muni – it was a beautiful morning, there was a cool breeze, but he was perspiring. But he was a sincere man. He did not stand up to contradict me, on the contrary, I received a messenger in the afternoon, who said, "Chandan Muni wants to meet you, and he's very sorry that he cannot come, because his committee will not allow it."

I said, "There is no problem. I am not imprisoned, my wings are not cut. I don't care about any committee, I can come."

So the messenger said, "First let me go and make arrangements so that you can meet in privacy."

I said, "What is the matter? Let others be there."

But he said, "You don't understand. Since this morning, Chandan Muni has been crying. He's seventy years old, and he became a monk when he was only twelve years old. His father became a monk, the mother had died – now where was this child to go? This was the most convenient thing, that he also became a monk with his father; so he became a monk. He has never known what life is, he has never played with children, he has never seen anything that can be called pleasant."

So I said, "Okay, you go ahead and make arrangements, I am coming." Still, a crowd gathered. They had been suspecting since the morning that something had happened to Chandan Muni – he was not speaking and his eyes were full of tears. He had to beg of the crowd, "Please, leave the two of us alone!"

He locked the doors, and he said to me, "It was hard to hear your words, they were like arrows going directly into my heart; but whatever you said is true. I am not as courageous as I should be, and that's why I don't want anybody else to hear this, but I have not known life. I have not known anything. I have only learned from scriptures – they are empty. And now at the age of seventy, what do you suggest for me to do?"

I said, "I think the first thing is to open the doors and let the people come in. Of what are you afraid? You don't have anything to lose. You have never lived – you died at the age of twelve. Now, a dead man has nothing to lose. But let them listen. They have been worshipping you; just because of their worship your ego was fulfilled and you managed to live this torturous life, this horrible nightmare that religions have called saintliness – it is simply pathology."

He was hesitant, but still he gathered courage and opened the doors. And when the people heard that he knew nothing, rather than praising his honesty and sincerity, they all started condemning him, saying, "You have been cheating us!" They threw him out of their temple.

For truth it seems there is no home, but for hypocrisy, all worship, all respectability, is available.

This hermit reminds me of Chandan Muni. I don't know what happened to him, but whatever may have happened must have been better than what had been happening before. At least he sacrificed his respectability for being sincere, for being truthful, and this is a big step.

The hermit is asking: *Speak to us of Pleasure.* The word *pleasure* is without any meaning for the hermit; he has heard only condemnation of it. He may have himself been condemning it, but he has never tasted it.

I would like to tell you a beautiful story. One day in paradise, in one of the Zorba the Buddha restaurants, Gautam Buddha, Confucius, and Lao Tzu were sitting and chit-chatting. A beautiful naked woman came with a big jug and asked the three, "Would you like to have some juice of life?"

Buddha immediately closed his eyes. He said, "Be ashamed of yourself! You are trying to degrade us. With great effort and arduous austerities, somehow we have reached here, and you have brought the juice of life. Get lost!" And he said all these things with closed eyes.

But Confucius kept his eyes half open, half closed. That's his whole philosophy: the golden mean – neither this extreme nor that extreme. He said, "I would like to have a little taste, because without tasting it I cannot say anything about it." She poured some juice of life into a cup. Confucius just sipped it, gave it back to her, and said, "It is very bitter."

Lao Tzu said, "Give me the whole jug." The woman said, "The whole jug? Are you going to drink from the jug?" He said, "That's my approach to life: unless you have drunk it in its totality you cannot say anything about it. It may be bitter in the beginning, it may be sweet in the end – who knows?"

Before the woman could say anything he took the jug away and just drank, in one single breath, the whole juice of life. He said, "Confucius, you are wrong. Everything needs a certain training in taste. It was bitter because it was unknown to you; it was bitter because you were already prejudiced against it. Your whole talk about the golden mean is empty philosophy. I can say that the more I drank of it, the sweeter it became. First it was only pleasant; in the end it became ecstatic."

Buddha could not stand this praise of life. He simply stood up and moved out of the Zorba the Buddha restaurant. Lao Tzu said, "What happened to this fellow? He has been sitting with closed eyes. In the first place, there is no need to close your eyes, the woman is so beautiful. If there was something ugly you can close your eyes, it is understandable, but to close your eyes to such a beautiful woman is to show insensitivity, is to show humiliation, condemnation, is to show some deep-rooted fear. Perhaps that fellow is very repressed, and he is afraid his repression may surface."

Confucius was not ready to listen to Lao Tzu because he was going too far from the golden mean, so he left. And Lao Tzu started dancing. I have heard he is still dancing...

Life has to be lived before you decide anything about it – for or against. Those who have lived it in its intensity and totality have never been against it. Those who have been against it are the people who have never lived it in its intensity, who have never allowed it their totality; they have kept themselves aloof and closed – but that's what the religions have been teaching, and how they have been destroying humanity.

Almustafa replied:

Pleasure is a freedom-song...

The statements he is going to make are very significant:

Pleasure is a freedom-song,
But it is not freedom.

Pleasure is only a song, a by-product; when you know freedom the song will arise in you. But they are not synonymous. The song may remain silent – it depends.

You feel pleasure only when you are living a moment of freedom – freedom from care, freedom from worries, freedom from concerns, freedom from jealousies, freedom from everything. In that moment of absolute freedom a song arises in you, and that song is pleasure. Freedom is the mother, the song is only one of the children; there are many other children to the mother. So they are not synonymous. Freedom brings many flowers – it is only one of those flowers. And freedom brings many treasures – it is only one of those treasures.

It is the blossoming of your desires,
But it is not their fruit.

Flowers are beautiful. You can enjoy them, appreciate them, but they cannot nourish you, they cannot become your food. You can have them for decoration, but they cannot become your blood, your bones and your marrow. This is what he means: *It is the blossoming of your desires, but it is not their fruit.*

So don't stop at pleasure, there is much more ahead. Enjoy the flowers, collect the flowers, make a garland of the flowers, but remember: there are fruits also. And the fruit of your ripening is not pleasure; the fruit is blissfulness.

Pleasure is only a beginning – the tree is ready. The flowers are a song to announce that the tree is pregnant, and soon the fruits will be coming.

Don't get lost in pleasures, but don't escape from them either. Enjoy them, but remember, there is much more to life than pleasure.

Life does not end with pleasure, it only begins with it; the fruit is blissfulness. But pleasure gives you some taste of what is going to be ahead. It gives you a dream, a longing for more; it is a promise, "Just wait, fruits will be coming. Don't close your eyes to the flowers; otherwise you will never find the fruits."

That's what I have been telling you again and again, in different ways. My words may be different, but my song is the same. I may enter the temple from different doors, but it is the same temple.

Zorba is only a flower, Buddha is the fruit. Unless you have both you are not complete, something is missing; there will always remain a gap in your heart, a dark corner in your soul. Unless Buddha and Zorba dance together in your being – the flower and the fruit, the beginning and the end – you will not know the real meaning of existence.

The meaning of existence has not to be searched for by your intellect, it has to be experienced in life.

It is a depth calling unto a height...

Pleasure is a depth calling unto a height. Remember always that every depth is always close to a height; only the sunlit tops of mountains have deep valleys by their side. Pleasure is in the valleys, but if you have known pleasure it will create, it will stir in your being, the longing for that faraway sunlit peak. If the darkness is so beautiful, if the valley is so fulfilling, how can you contain your temptation to reach to the heights? When the depths give so much, you have to explore the heights.

Pleasure is a tremendous temptation to reach to the heights. It is not against your spiritual growth; it is a friend, not a foe. And those who have denied it have denied the heights also, because the heights and the valleys exist together. The valleys have their own beauty, there is nothing sinful about them, there is nothing evil about them – just don't get lost. Enjoy, but remain alert, because there is much more. And you should not be content with the darkness of the valley. The pleasure creates in you a spiritual discontent: if darkness can give so much, can yield so much, what about the heights?

It is a depth calling unto a height,
But it is not the deep nor the high.

Pleasure itself is more like plain ground. On one side is the high peak of the mountain; because of the height of the mountain it seems to be the depth, but really it is plain ground.

There are depths and there are heights. If you fall into the depths, you will be falling into a painful existence, into anguish – below pleasure is pain, agony. Above pleasure is blissfulness, ecstasy.

It is unfortunate that millions of very nice people have renounced pleasure and fallen into the dark, bottomless hole of pain, misery, austerity; but they go on consoling themselves because their scriptures go on telling them that the more you suffer, the more you will gain after life. Nobody tells them, "There is no need to wait for a paradise after life. Don't go against pleasure, but follow the pleasure into its totality and it will start leading you, by and by, upward toward the heights."

Here you can be in hell, you can be in heaven; it all depends on you, where you are moving. Don't move against pleasure; let pleasure be your arrow moving toward the stars.

It is the caged taking wing...

In pleasure, the caged bird grows wings, but still it is in the cage; now it has wings, but it has not the sky available to it. It can be said, "Pleasure is caged blissfulness."

Blissfulness is pleasure on the wing, rising higher into the sky. When pleasure becomes free from all prisons it goes through a transmutation, a transformation. It has the seed in it, somebody just has to remind it, "You are containing tremendous potential." It has wings, but is not aware of its wings.

To be with a master is not to learn something. To be with a master is to be infected by something. Seeing the master on the wing, in the air, suddenly you become aware, "I have also got the same wings." The master becomes a remembrance. It is not a teaching that a master transfers, it is a remembrance that he invokes.

It is the caged taking wing,
But it is not space encompassed.

So those who know pleasure have become acquainted with their wings; now they have to find their way out of the cage. And the cage is your own, homemade. It is your jealousy, which you go on feeding; it is your competitiveness, which you go on giving energy to; it is your own ego, which you don't drop but go on carrying, howsoever heavy the burden is. The cage is not somebody else's; hence it is very easy to drop it.

It happened to one of the Sufi mystics, al-Hillaj Mansoor... I love the man very much. There have been many mystics, and there will be many mystics, but I don't think anybody will have the same taste as al-Hillaj Mansoor. He was rare in every sense. For example, somebody asked him, "How to be free? You all go on talking about freedom, freedom – but *how* to be free?"

He said, "It is very simple, just see." They were sitting in a mosque with pillars like these. Al-Hillaj went close to a pillar, caught hold of the pillar with both hands, and started shouting, "Help me! How can I be free from this pillar?"

The man said, "Don't be mad, you yourself are clinging to the pillar. Nobody is doing anything, neither is the pillar doing anything. What nonsense are you doing?"

He said, "I am simply answering you. You had asked me how to be free. Have you ever asked anybody the art of not being free? That you know perfectly well. You go on creating new chains, new bondages – it is your own doing. Undo it! And it is good that it is your own doing, because you can undo it without anybody else's permission."

Still, al-Hillaj was holding the pillar. The man said, "At least now I have understood the point, but please leave that pillar because a crowd is gathering. Everybody knows you are mad, but I am feeling embarrassed to be with you!"

He said, "Only if you have really understood will I leave this pillar, otherwise I will die with this pillar."

He said, "My God, to ask you a question is to create trouble."

And the crowd started abusing the person. They said, "Why did you disturb al-Hillaj? What kind of question have you asked?"

He said, "It is strange, I had asked a simple question, How to be free? Rather than answering he went to the pillar, and he's holding the pillar, and he's shouting for help. That's why you have all gathered."

And al-Hillaj was still shouting, "Help me! How can I be free?"

Finally, the man said, "Forgive me, I will try, but don't make too much mockery of me. Leave that pillar!"

He said, "What do you think? – am I holding the pillar or is the pillar holding me?"

The man said, "Mansoor, although you have become a great mystic we were boyhood friends, we studied in the same school; just remember our friendship before this whole crowd. Now the whole town is here and they are all angry with me. This is not the way to answer a question. I was asking a philosophical question."

Mansoor said, "Philosophical question? Then you should not come to a man like me. Philosophy is only for fools. Only those who are really in search of truth should enter my house. This is the house of God. And I have answered you. If you want to be free, you can be free this very moment, because you are holding all your chains as if they are not chains but ornaments. Drop them! Even if they are made of gold, they are not allowing you to be free, and they are not allowing your wings to open in the air."

Ay, in very truth, pleasure is a freedom-song.
And I fain would have you sing it with fullness of heart...

Man has completely forgotten one thing – fullness. He loves, but there is not fullness of the heart. He weeps, but the tears are shallow, perhaps only a formality. He smiles, because he is expected to smile.

I have heard about a boss, and he knew no more than three jokes. But every day he would collect his whole office – all the clerks, head clerks – and he would tell one of those jokes. And they all would laugh as if they had never heard it. They had to, because not to laugh was an insult to the boss.

One day one woman typist did not laugh, and the boss said, "What is the matter. Why are you not laughing?"

She said, "I am resigning; I have got another job. Why should I laugh?"

People are laughing out of formality, respectfulness, but this kind of laugh cannot be wholehearted. None of your actions is total: that is your misery, that is your hell.

A king had come to see a Zen master. The Zen master had a beautiful garden and, just in front of the gate, an old man was chopping wood. The king asked him, "Can I ask, who are you?"

He said, "Who am I? You can see – a woodcutter."

He said, "That's true, that I can see, but I have come to see your master."

He said, "My master? I don't have any master."

The king thought, this man seems to be mad. But just to

complete the conversation he said, "But is this a Zen monastery?"

The man said, "Maybe."

So the king moved ahead. When he reached the house deep inside the forest he entered the house and he saw the same wood-cutter, wearing the robe of a Zen monk, sitting in a Zen posture, looking really beautiful and graceful. The king looked at his face. He said, "What is going on? Do you have a twin brother?"

He said, "Perhaps."

The king said, "Who is cutting wood in front of the gate?"

He said, "Whoever is cutting wood, he is a woodcutter. What business is it to talk about a woodcutter? I am a master."

The king was very puzzled, but the master said, "Don't feel puzzled. When I am cutting wood, I am a woodcutter; I don't leave any space for anything else. And when I am a master, I am a master. You have not met two persons, you have met one person who is always total. Next time you may find me fishing in the pond, then you will meet a fisherman. Whatever I do, I *am* my action, in my totality."

Moment to moment, living life in totality, is my whole teaching. Those who have known life and its mysteries are agreed upon one point: that you should be full of heart, whatever you are doing.

Kahlil Gibran is saying: *And I fain would have you sing it with fullness of heart...* When the song of freedom happens to you, let your whole heart dance, sing.

...yet I would not have you lose your hearts in the singing.

This is a very strange, but significant, statement. It seems to be contradictory. He is saying, "Sing the song with the fullness of your heart, but still remain alert. Don't get lost, don't stop witnessing."

When your action is total and the witness is silently watching it, you will not only find the song of pleasure, you will also find something far greater, which we have been calling blissfulness. Blissfulness comes with the witness.

Pleasure needs totality – but don't get lost into it, otherwise you will have stopped at pleasure and will not move higher than that.

Some of your youth seek pleasure as if it were all, and they are judged and rebuked.

...of course, by the old. The swift and the strong and the bold of step are always condemned by the crippled, criticized in many ways. It is a cover-up. The crippled person cannot accept that he is crippled, and he cannot accept that somebody else is not crippled. To cover his inferiority he starts condemning, criticizing.

The old people are continuously condemning the young seekers of pleasure, judging them as sinners, although deep down in their own being they would like still to be young.

Some of your youth seek pleasure as if it were all... It is wrong to think that pleasure is all, but it is also wrong to judge and condemn them. The man who condemns them is deep down hankering for the same thing, but finds himself weaker, older, no longer adequate enough.

The wiser man will say, "Seek pleasure, there is no harm in it. But remember this is not all – because I have known higher things, better things. But I will not stop you from seeking, seek with the fullness of your heart! In that very fullness of the heart and that very search and the experience of pleasure, perhaps you may start looking for something higher, something better; something more alive, more beautiful, more immortal."

The wise man never condemns – that is the criterion of a wise man – and those who condemn are simply *other*wise, not wise.

I would not judge nor rebuke them. I would have them seek.

Kahlil Gibran has an immense treasure of wisdom.

I would not judge nor rebuke them. I would have them seek.
For they shall find pleasure, but not her alone;
Seven are her sisters, and the least of them is more beautiful than pleasure.

Here he has referred to the Eastern tradition of Tantra, which talks about seven *chakras* – seven centers of your growth. This is something to be very carefully understood. Perhaps people who have been reading Kahlil Gibran may have never bothered about who the seven sisters are, and even if they had thought about them, I don't think... Unless they know something about Tantra and the Eastern findings of the inner ladder of growth, they will not be able to understand.

In the university where I used to teach, there were many professors who loved Kahlil Gibran, and I have asked many of them, "Can you say something to me about the seven sisters?"

They said, "Seven sisters? I know nothing about them."

I said, "What kind of reading do you do?"

Kahlil Gibran is saying: ...*and the least of them is more beautiful than pleasure.*"

They used to say to me, "You read things in a strange way. We have passed this sentence, but the question never arose. Now that you ask, we also wonder who the seven sisters are." The people in the West will certainly be unaware. If even in the East they don't know who the seven sisters are, what to say about the West?

Tantra talks about seven centers – and pleasure is not even the first center. Pleasure is below the first center. Pleasure is a biological phenomenon; it is your sexuality. It uses your energy, but it is bondage with biology. Biology wants you to reproduce children, because biology knows you are not dependable. You can pop off any moment!

Biology has its own ways to keep the stream of life flowing. If there were no pleasure in sexual experiences, I don't think any man or any woman would reproduce children; then the whole thing would look so stupid, such strange gymnastics. All women are aware of it, only men are not so aware. While making love, women want to put the light off but the man wants the light on. It is very strange to find a woman who keeps her eyes open while making love, she closes her eyes – let this idiot do whatsoever he feels. If there were no pleasure... It is a trick and a strategy of biology – just like giving a chocolate to a child; a little pleasure so you can suffer the gymnastics. And slowly, slowly you become so accustomed to the chocolate...

Above the pleasure center is the first chakra, which sometimes – very rarely – is experienced by accident. People are not aware of the whole science of Tantra; otherwise everybody would be able to understand the first center very easily. Just the small pleasure of making love does not take you to the first center, but if your lovemaking brings an orgasmic explosion...

But people are so quick in making love! This quickness in making love is a by-product of your religious upbringing, because they have been condemning sex. They have not been able to destroy it, but they have certainly succeeded in making it short. They have not been able to destroy it completely, but they have poisoned it. So even when people in love are making love, both feel ashamed as if they are doing something ugly, so the quicker it ends the better!

For biological purposes it is perfectly okay – biology is not interested in your orgasmic experience. But if you can prolong the process of lovemaking, if you can make it a meditation, silent, beautiful, if you make it something sacred... Before making love take a bath, and when you enter your bedroom enter with the same feeling as when you enter a temple. It is a temple of love, but in the temple of love, people are fighting, quarreling, nagging, throwing pillows at each other, shouting, screaming; you destroy the whole atmosphere.

You should burn incense, you should play some beautiful music, you should dance. You should not be in a hurry to make love – that should be the climax of your whole game. You should meditate together, you should be silent together, you should dance together. In this dance, in this togetherness, in this singing, with the incense, you must create in your bedroom a temple, and only then...

You should not make an effort to make love; let it happen spontaneously, on its own accord. If it does not happen, there is no need to worry – you enjoyed the meditation, you enjoyed the dance, you enjoyed the music. It has been a beautiful experience, leave it.

Your love should not be an action, it should be a spontaneous phenomenon that surprises you. Only in that spontaneity can love become orgasmic. And the moment love becomes orgasmic you have reached the first chakra, you have met the first sister – which is far more beautiful than pleasure.

The first three chakras are self-centered: the first is unconscious orgasmic pleasure; the second is half conscious, half asleep; the third is fully conscious orgasmic pleasure. In the third your love and your meditation meet.

The next three... The fourth is the heart center. Only at the fourth is the beginning of a new world – the world of love. Below the fourth it was only refinement of sexual energy; with the fourth you transcend sex completely. There is no more refinement. You have entered into a new kind of energy, qualitatively different from sex. It is the same energy, but so refined that the very refinement makes it a totally new phenomenon.

At the fourth center, when you are entering into love you can feel it but you cannot express it. It is so new you don't have any words. It is so unknown and so sudden that time stops, mind stops. You are suddenly in a silence that you have never dreamed of before.

With the fifth center, expression comes into being: love becomes creativity. It may find expression in different ways in different people – it may become music, it may become poetry, it may become a sculpture, it may become dance – infinite are the possibilities. But one thing is certain: when you are at the fifth center, love becomes creative.

Below the first center love was only productive – productive of children. At the fifth center it becomes creative; you create new kinds of children. For the poet, his poetry is his child; for the musician, his music is his child. At the fifth center everybody becomes a mother, a womb.

These two centers, the fourth and the fifth, are centered on the other. The first three were centered on your own self: that's why sex is never a fulfillment and sex is always a quarrel, a fight. It creates intimate enemies, not friends, because both partners are self-centered. They want to get more and more pleasure from the other. Both are wanting; nobody is ready to give.

The fourth and fifth change the direction: from getting, the transformation is toward giving. Hence, in love there is no quarrel, no jealousy, no fight. It gives freedom. It is creative – it creates something beautiful for the other, for the beloved. It may be painting, it may be music, it may be a beautiful garden, but the center is the beloved. It is not for one's own pleasure, it is for the happiness and pleasure of the other. If the other is happy, one is happy.

With the sixth center your energy enters again into a new experience. In Tantra it is called "the opening of the third eye." It is only a symbol. It means you have now attained a clarity of vision, you can see without any hindrance; there are no longer any curtains on your eyes, nothing hinders your vision. You can see without any projection, you can see things as they are, in their truth, in their beauty; it is not that you are projecting something. Before this center, everybody is projecting.

Of course, there are people who will not be able to enjoy classical music, because they have been trained to project... They can only enjoy modern, contemporary, Western music – which to the real musical person is nothing but insane noise, a kind of neurosis. People are jumping and screaming, from the Beatles to the skinheads – it is all insanity, it is not music. But to enjoy classical music, you need a certain discipline.

If you want to enjoy the music of the wind passing through the pine trees you will need a clarity, a silence; you are not expecting anything, you are not projecting anything.

With the opening of the third eye you are no longer separate from the other. At the first three centers you were self-centered; with the two other centers you were other-oriented. With the sixth you become one with the other – there is no longer separation. Lovers start feeling a kind of synchronicity. Their heartbeats have the same rhythm, they start understanding each other without saying a single word.

With the seventh, that is the highest man can rise in the body – it is called *sahasrar*, the seventh center of your being – you become one with the whole universe. First you become one with your beloved at the sixth center; at the seventh you become one with the ultimate, with the whole. These are the seven sisters that Kahlil Gibran is mentioning, and this is the whole spectrum of spiritual growth.

Have you not heard of the man who was digging in the earth for roots and found a treasure?

It is an ancient proverb in Lebanon. A man was digging for roots; he was so hungry he could not afford even to buy fruit, so he was digging for roots to eat. But he found a treasure. Referring to it, Kahlil Gibran is saying, "We started by digging for roots – pleasure; but if you go on digging, you may find treasures beyond treasures."

It is a fact established by all the mystics of the East that with the seventh you become absolutely free from all prisons, from all thoughts, from all religions, from all ideologies; with the seventh, your cage has disappeared.

Now you can breathe in the open sky and you can fly to the stars.

About Osho

Osho defies categorization. His thousands of talks cover everything from the individual quest for meaning to the most urgent social and political issues facing society today. Osho's books are not written but are transcribed from audio and video recordings of his extemporaneous talks to international audiences. As he puts it, "So remember: whatever I am saying is not just for you... I am talking also for the future generations."

Osho has been described by *The Sunday Times* in London as one of the "1000 Makers of the 20th Century" and by American author Tom Robbins as "the most dangerous man since Jesus Christ." *Sunday Mid-Day* (India) has selected Osho as one of ten people – along with Gandhi, Nehru and Buddha – who have changed the destiny of India.

About his own work Osho has said that he is helping to create the conditions for the birth of a new kind of human being. He often characterizes this new human being as "Zorba the Buddha" – capable both of enjoying the earthy pleasures of a Zorba the Greek and the silent serenity of a Gautama the Buddha.

Running like a thread through all aspects of Osho's talks and meditations is a vision that encompasses both the timeless wisdom of all ages past and the highest potential of today's (and tomorrow's) science and technology.

Osho is known for his revolutionary contribution to the science of inner transformation, with an approach to meditation that acknowledges the accelerated pace of contemporary life. His unique OSHO Active Meditations are designed to first release the accumulated stresses of body and mind, so that it is then easier to take an experience of stillness and thought-free relaxation into daily life.

Two autobiographical works by the author are available:
Autobiography of a Spiritually Incorrect Mystic,
St Martins Press, New York (book and eBook)
Glimpses of a Golden Childhood,
OSHO Media International, Pune, India

OSHO International Meditation Resort

Location
Located 100 miles southeast of Mumbai in the thriving modern city of Pune, India, the OSHO International Meditation Resort is a holiday destination with a difference. The Meditation Resort is spread over 28 acres of spectacular gardens in a beautiful tree-lined residential area.

Uniqueness
Each year the Meditation Resort welcomes thousands of people from more than 100 countries. The unique campus provides an opportunity for a direct personal experience of a new way of living – with more awareness, relaxation, celebration and creativity. A great variety of around-the-clock and around-the-year program options are available. Doing nothing and just relaxing is one of them!

All programs are based on the OSHO vision of "Zorba the Buddha" – a qualitatively new kind of human being who is able *both* to participate creatively in everyday life *and* to relax into silence and meditation.

OSHO Meditations
A full daily schedule of meditations for every type of person includes methods that are active and passive, traditional and revolutionary, and in particular the OSHO Active Meditations™. The meditations take place in what must be the world's largest meditation hall, the OSHO Auditorium.

OSHO Multiversity
Individual sessions, courses and workshops cover everything from creative arts to holistic health, personal transformation, relationship and life transition, work-as-meditation, esoteric sciences, and the "Zen" approach to sports and recreation. The secret of the OSHO Multiversity's success lies in the fact that all its programs are combined with meditation, supporting the understanding that as human beings we are far more than the sum of our parts.

OSHO Basho Spa

The luxurious Basho Spa provides for leisurely open-air swimming surrounded by trees and tropical green. The uniquely styled, spacious Jacuzzi, the saunas, gym, tennis courts...all these are enhanced by their stunningly beautiful setting.

Cuisine

A variety of different eating areas serve delicious Western, Asian and Indian vegetarian food – most of it organically grown especially for the Meditation Resort. Breads and cakes are baked in the resort's own bakery.

Night life

There are many evening events to choose from – dancing being at the top of the list! Other activities include full-moon meditations beneath the stars, variety shows, music performances and meditations for daily life.

Or you can just enjoy meeting people at the Plaza Café, or walking in the nighttime serenity of the gardens of this fairytale environment.

Facilities

You can buy all your basic necessities and toiletries in the Galleria. The Multimedia Gallery sells a large range of OSHO media products. There is also a bank, a travel agency and a Cyber Café on-campus. For those who enjoy shopping, Pune provides all the options, ranging from traditional and ethnic Indian products to all of the global brand-name stores.

Accommodation

You can choose to stay in the elegant rooms of the OSHO Guesthouse, or for longer stays opt for one of the OSHO Living-In program packages. Additionally there is a plentiful variety of nearby hotels and serviced apartments.

www.osho.com/meditationresort
www.osho.com/guesthouse
www.osho.com/livingin

More Books and eBooks by OSHO Media International

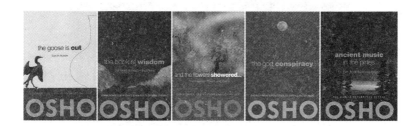

The God Conspiracy:
The Path from Superstition to Super Consciousness

Discover the Buddha: 53 Meditations to Meet the Buddha Within
Gold Nuggets: Messages from Existence

OSHO Classics
The Book of Wisdom: The Heart of Tibetan Buddhism.
The Mustard Seed: The Revolutionary Teachings of Jesus
Ancient Music in the Pines: In Zen, Mind Suddenly Stops
The Empty Boat: Encounters with Nothingness
A Bird on the Wing: Zen Anecdotes for Everyday Life
The Path of Yoga: Discovering the Essence and Origin of Yoga
And the Flowers Showered: The Freudian Couch and Zen
Nirvana: The Last Nightmare: Learning to Trust in Life
The Goose Is Out: Zen in Action
Absolute Tao: Subtle Is the Way to Love, Happiness and Truth

The Tantra Experience: Evolution through Love
Tantric Transformation: When Love Meets Meditation

Pillars of Consciousness (illustrated)
BUDDHA: His Life and Teachings and Impact on Humanity
ZEN: Its History and Teachings and Impact on Humanity
TANTRA: The Way of Acceptance
TAO: The State and the Art

Authentic Living

Danger: Truth at Work: The Courage to Accept the Unknowable
The Magic of Self-Respect: Awakening to Your Own Awareness
Born With a Question Mark in Your Heart

OSHO eBooks and "OSHO-Singles"

Emotions: Freedom from Anger, Jealousy & Fear
Meditation: The First and Last Freedom
What is Meditation?
The Book of Secrets: 112 Meditations to Discover the Mystery Within

20 Difficult Things to Accomplish in this World
Compassion, Love and Sex
Hypnosis in the Service of Meditation
Why Is Communication So Difficult, Particularly Between Lovers?
Bringing Up Children
Why Should I Grieve Now?: facing a loss and letting it go
Love and Hate: just two sides of the same coin

Next Time You Feel Angry...
Next Time You Feel Lonely...
Next Time You Feel Suicidal...

OSHO Media BLOG
http://oshomedia.blog.osho.com

For More Information

www. **OSHO** .com

a comprehensive multi-language website including a magazine, OSHO Books, OSHO Talks in audio and video formats, the OSHO Library text archive in English and Hindi and extensive information about OSHO Meditations. You will also find the program schedule of the OSHO Multiversity and information about the OSHO International Meditation Resort.

http://OSHO.com/AllAboutOSHO
http://OSHO.com/Resort
http://OSHO.com/Shop
http://www.youtube.com/OSHO
http://www.Twitter.com/OSHO
http://www.facebook.com/pages/OSHO.International

To contact OSHO International Foundation:
www.osho.com/oshointernational,
oshointernational@oshointernational.com